FERMENTAL

The Art of & Obsession with Fermented Foods & Drinks

FAITH CANTER

EMPOWERED
BOOKS

Published in 2022 by Empowered Books

Copyright © Faith Canter 2022

Faith Canter has asserted her right to be identified as the author of this Work in accordance with the Copyright, Designs and Patents Act 1988

ISBN Paperback: 978-0-9957047-8-7
Ebook: 978-0-9957047-9-4

All rights reserved. No part of this publication may be reproduced, stored in a retrieval system, or transmitted in any form or by any means, electronic, mechanical, photocopying, recording or otherwise, without the prior permission of the copyright owner.

A CIP catalogue copy of this book can be found in the British Library.

Published with the help of Indie Authors World
www.indieauthorsworld.com

Dedication

Dear Dad & Mum (AKA Pete & Pat),

There are so many, many things I am deeply grateful for from growing up with you as my parents!

For the long walks along the cliffs, where you taught us about plants, birds, bees, butterflies, and nature. I rejoice in those learnings and those precious moments as a family. For the freedom to be children, to grow, to get dirty, to learn from our mistakes (for which there were many) and to stay out all day messing about in quarries and on cliff sides. We ate fresh and often homegrown food and we camped out in tents in the garden. We knew we did not have much financially, but we had so much else that meant so much more. We were free, but we were deeply loved and we learnt about things that really matter.

I know you sometimes felt you had failed us, but you never ever did. We always had everything we really needed in life, we were happy and healthy, dirty and annoying, and we knew we were loved.

Everything we have been through we needed to go through, to end up who and where we are now.

Through every challenge I have grown. Through every rejection I've found a redirection. Through every loss I have found more of myself. And through every pain I've become stronger and more me.

I am the person I am now, because of everything you gave and did not give me. You were and still are the most perfect parents for me on this crazy-ass path of life!

You gave us everything that was needed to be us, and we are kind of alright now, no?? ;0)

With deep love and appreciation to you both xxxx

Contents

About the Author	11
The Benefits of Fermented Foods & Drinks	15
Introduction: What are Fermented Foods & Drink?	19
Fermenting Tips	23
How You Can Support Your Detoxing Journey	29
Sauerkrauts	**31**
Basic Sauerkraut	33
Rainbow Sauerkraut	35
Red Cabbage & Ginger Sauerkraut	36
Golden Sauerkraut	37
Celeriac & Ginger Sauerkraut	38
Beetroot & Ginger Sauerkraut	39
Curried Squash Sauerkraut	40
Courgette & Turmeric Sauerkraut	41
Christmas Sauerkraut	42
Indian Sauerkraut	43
Nettle, Garlic & Fenugreek Sauerkraut	45
Curtido	46
Kimchi	**47**
Basic Kimchi	48
Golden or Curried Kimchi	50
Miso Kimchi	51
Kimchi Kraut	52
Carrot Kimchi	53
Chunky Carrot & Radish Kimchi	54
Un-spiced Kimchi	55

Veggies — 57

- Piccalilli — 58
- Pickles — 59
- Curried Cauliflower — 60
- Peppers — 62
- 'Pickled' Onions — 63
- Carrot and Garlic Sticks — 64
- Parsnip & Carrot Sticks — 65
- Salsa — 66
- Pineapple & Papaya Salsa — 67
- Garlic Mushrooms — 69
- Onion Relish — 70
- Spicy Fermented Aubergine Dip — 71
- Tomato, Basil and Garlic — 72

Extras — 73

- Sourdough — 74
- Cashew 'Cheese' — 76
- Pumpkin Seed 'Cheese' — 78
- Wild Garlic Pesto — 79
- Mayonnaise — 80
- Ketchup — 81
- Kombucha Mustard — 82
- Chili Sauce — 83
- Mango Chutney — 84
- Zhug — 86
- Kidney Bean Pate — 87
- Black Bean Miso — 89
- Tapenade — 90
- Honey Garlic — 91
- Spicy Lemons — 92
- Breakfast Ferment — 94
- Spicy Pineapple — 95

Fermented Drinks　　　　　　　　　　　　　　　　　97

　Kombucha　　　　　　　　　　　　　　　　　　　99
　Water Kefir　　　　　　　　　　　　　　　　　　102
　Milk Kefir　　　　　　　　　　　　　　　　　　　103
　Ginger Bug　　　　　　　　　　　　　　　　　　104
　Ginger Beer　　　　　　　　　　　　　　　　　　105
　Turmeric Mead　　　　　　　　　　　　　　　　106
　Tepache　　　　　　　　　　　　　　　　　　　　107
　Beetroot Kvass　　　　　　　　　　　　　　　　109
　Christmas Kvass　　　　　　　　　　　　　　　　110
　Grapefruit Juice　　　　　　　　　　　　　　　　111
　Apple Juice　　　　　　　　　　　　　　　　　　112
　Apple Cider Vinegar　　　　　　　　　　　　　　113

Fermented Skin Care　　　　　　　　　　　　　　115

　Kombucha Toner　　　　　　　　　　　　　　　116
　Kefir Face Mask for Combination Skin　　　　　117
　Kombucha Face Mask　　　　　　　　　　　　　119
　Face & Body Scrub　　　　　　　　　　　　　　120
　Kombucha Hair Tonic　　　　　　　　　　　　　121
　Rice Water Shampoo　　　　　　　　　　　　　122
　Scalp Scrub　　　　　　　　　　　　　　　　　　123

Fermented Cleaning Products　　　　　　　　　125

　Surface Cleaner　　　　　　　　　　　　　　　　126
　Oven Cleaner　　　　　　　　　　　　　　　　　127

Art & Obsession　　　　　　　　　　　　　　　　129

About the Author

Hey, I'm Faith, a Scottish-born, forty-something, dyslexic, English language- and grammar- confounded author, brought up on the south coast of England and now living off-grid in central Portugal with her growing clan of animals. That is what first sprang to mind when I sat down to write this section. When I sat down to tell you who I am, how I came to be and why I am some sort of 'expert' in the field of fermenting.

But that tells you nothing, nothing of the struggles and the strifes, nothing of the losses, learnings and loves, and nothing of why I started to get my ferment-on, some 12+ years ago.

I know this is a 'cook' or maybe I should say 'uncook' book, so maybe you were not expecting to get to know me at all. However, I feel it is important for you to understand I was once (well for more than half of my short life) struggling greatly with my mental and physical health, and with the assistance of fermented foods and drinks I no longer am.

I was lost, lost in a sea of feeling incredibly ill almost all the time and also thinking this is how everyone felt and there was not much I could do about it. But, as the trips to the hospital got more frequent and as the chronic irritable bowel syndrome (IBS), food intolerances, sensitivities, fatigue, pain, depression and anxiety got worse, I thought this isn't right and there must be another way. There must be something else I could do other than taking medications that weren't helping, taking supplements that I was not absorbing, or avoiding the huge and ever-growing list of foods and drinks that my body was reacting to.

It seemed that the medical and also alternative routes were all just putting plasters over the symptoms, rather than looking at the root cause of the issue. Sometimes I would feel a little better, but most of the time I'd feel a lot worse and I just had to deal with it. Well, I was done with that silly game!

I started doing more research on gut health, not just the supplements to take but researching what could be causing the IBS and food intolerances etc., and especially why it was getting worse as the years rolled on.

I realised that through legal (and probably non-legal) drug use, especially antibiotics, contraceptive pills and steroids over the years, plus a huge dollop of stress, anxiety and depression, I had severally compromised the health of my digestive system and thus pretty much every other system of the body. Despite what I'd been told by everyone else that I had sought advice from, there was indeed many things I could do to address and *recover* from this imbalance instead of just managing it.

I realised that my digestive system was seriously depleted of good bacteria, and that addressing this imbalance alone wouldn't just have a huge impact on my digestive health, but would also help the health of my whole body and mind too.

I came across these weird things called fermented foods and drinks that claimed to be jam-packed with good bacteria, probiotics and nutrients, which would also assist in detoxing you from all the bad stuff too. Really? Was I prepared to eat these strange looking, smelling and sometimes mouldy things? Sure I was! I was totally desperate and things needed to change. However, by this point I was seriously ill with chronic fatigue syndrome too and was often bed-bound, with no energy for bathing half the time let alone making this weirdness. So, to start with I bought them (the unpasteurised ones from health food shops, not the pasteurised rubbish from the supermarkets) and my husband (at the time) helped make them.

I admit I did not notice a difference right away (unfortunately), but it all made so much sense to me, so I continued on, consuming as many different varieties as possible and as often as possible. To start with I think I maybe had too much, because I sometimes thought I was intolerant to them too because I was running off to the toilet so frequently. But I found out that this is one of the things fermented foods and drinks is great at – detoxing! I took a little less instead and soon these side effects settled down, so I slowly built up how much I was having again.

After some time, maybe a few months, I realised I could tolerate a few more of the foods and drinks that I wasn't able to before. My reactions to certain foods and drinks were not so severe and I was no longer dreading the after-effects of eating and drinking.

I do not believe that fermented foods and drinks was what 'healed' me of all my woes, but I certainly believe it formed a vital and integral part of my recovery to full health after over 20 years of being so ill.

Fermented foods and drinks have so many benefits to our bodies and minds and to the planet, I have listed just a few of them in the next section for you. I honestly believe if we all consumed fermented foods and drinks daily that we'd have A LOT less physical and mental health concerns.

These weird foods and drinks really and truly can revolutionise our health care 'system' and the health of our nearest and dearest too!

So, this, in brief is how I came to be a fermenting nut, or you could say *fermental*! What I have found is that I am not alone, there is a huge community (which is ever growing) of people out there just as obsessed with fermented foods and drinks as me.

Wishing you a plate full of yumminess and a belly full of good bacteria, Faith xx

For more information visit: www.faithcanter.com

The Benefits of Fermented Foods & Drinks

Fermented foods restore the balance of the gut.

Improving food intolerance, bloating, constipation, irritable bowel syndrome, leaky gut, poor absorption, yeast infections, candida, allergies, hay fever and even asthma.

Fermenting vegetables increases their nutritional content.

Most fruits and vegetables are already high in many different nutrients, but the fermentation process harnesses the vegetable's beneficial bacteria, enzymes and additional vitamins. This also increases the available nutrients you uptake as none are destroyed in the preparation of these foods unlike cooking/drying vegetables etc.

Lessens the load on the digestive system.

Your body has to do much less work to break down fermented foods because they become pre-digested by the fermentation process. Also, the boost of beneficial flora that's delivered to your gut helps elimination, which is not only key to digestive health but also for the body to detox itself.

Fermented foods heal the intestinal tract from damage and restore optimal health.

Our modern diet, even for those of us who try to "eat healthy", is composed of enormous amounts of refined and processed foods. These foods ravage the gut by blunting the villi (the little "fingers" that grab and process each bit of food) and killing off the beneficial bacteria, leaving the intestinal walls raw, inflamed and unable to efficiently absorb nutrients. Eating fermented foods can heal the gut by repopulating it with multiple strains of beneficial bacteria and creating a healthy pH balance.

Stimulates and supports the immune system.

Lactic acid bacteria fights off pathogenic bacteria, lowers the pH of the GI tract and enhances immunity, thus keeping us healthier and better able to fight infection.

They have been dubbed Nature's Prozac.

As they assist the body's production of serotonin.

Supports the endocrine system.

When we support gut health we support our hormones. By removing yeasts and parasites from the endocrine system, fermented foods and drinks really help it to work more effectively. Plus, the additional uptake of more nutrients is a big bonus too.

Fermented foods promote skin, hair & nail health.

Because fermented foods and drinks are supporting uptake, elimination and gut health they, by default, support skin, hair and nail health too. You can even use fermented drinks and your kombucha scoby in skin and hair care products.

Increases energy levels.

As you increase your consumption of fermented foods and drinks your energy levels may also increase, because you are healing many imbalances within many systems of the body. This is because these systems don't need as much energy to function as they did, and also because you are up taking more nutrients which means your body has more fuel to use.

Assists in reducing sugar cravings.

Mainly because you are getting lots of nutrients you need, but also because it's removing yeasts and parasites that make you crave the foods they feed on.

Fermented foods promote dental health.

Cavities, gingivitis, periodontitis and bad breath are all caused by harmful bacteria in our mouths. By eating fermented foods rich in lactic acid bacteria we improve our mouth health.

Can reduce blood pressure.

These foods and drinks have the potential to dilate the blood vessels due to the histamine levels of many fermented foods, leading to reduced blood pressure.

Helps dairy intolerances.

This deserves its own section because so many people struggle with this issue. Not only do fermented foods and drinks assist with healing the digestive system, the fermentation process itself can also pre-digest dairy products, meaning people with dairy issues can often tolerate fermented versions of dairy dishes. This is often the case with other foods too.

Creates conscious kitchen creators.

When you take the time to prepare and look after fermented foods and drinks, you are more conscious of the food you are putting into your body and how it is affecting your body too. This is increased if you also grow the veggies yourself first too.

You can ferment pretty much anything.

Make your own side dishes, salsa, dips, drinks, spreads, desserts, you name it, you can make a highly nutrient-dense, probiotic version of it.

It's cheap and easy to do.

Fermented foods and drinks require very little equipment and most of the ingredients are cheap, easy to get a hold of and you can also grow yourself. When they say healthy food is expensive food it's just not the case with most fermented foods and drinks.

Helping the environment.

When you ferment your own foods, you minimise food waste, landfill space and collection, packaging, shopping, fossil-fuels, chemicals, shipping and your own time and money.

Introduction:
What are Fermented Foods & Drink?

Fermenting food and drink is an ancient way of preserving food, which makes them more nutrient-dense and packs them full of probiotics, prebiotics, antioxidants, amino acids and enzymes; and has the added bonus of tasting delicious and giving food and drink the ability to be kept for many months or even years.

This form of preservation should not be confused with pickling, which is when food is preserved in vinegar and, although this too is a wonderful way to preserve food, this way of preservation (unless you make the vinegar yourself or buy unpasteurized) kills off the bacteria, including the good stuff, meaning it has no probiotic value (but is still full of nutrients). Although fermented foods and drinks will eventually turn to vinegar or even alcohol, they start off very differently.

Fermented foods are generally started with salt, water (or vegetable brine) and the good bacteria already present in the vegetables. Fermented drinks are more generally started with sugar, water and the good bacteria in the fruit or vegetable, or with a starter like kefir grains or a scoby (more about these later in the book). Some fermented foods and drinks are started with whey, or the juice of a previous batch of ferments, or even weirdness like koji grains, but these are less often and usually when you start to go deeper down the fermenting rabbit hole.

Some of the most popular fermented foods and drinks are wine, beer, yogurt, cheese, olives, sourdough, sauerkraut, kimchi, miso, tempeh, kombucha, kefir and kvass. In fact, these days you can pick them up from many supermarkets and corner shops all over the World. Just beware though that if they say they are pasteurised on them (as they do in many supermarkets) then they no longer have any probiotics in them. They heat them like this to keep them more 'shelf-stable', but in fact it destroys a lot of the goodness.

You can ferment almost any food, but things differ depending on the water and sugar content of the food.

Every area of the World has its own original ways it used to ferment, and it's really lovely to explore and try these out as they differ dramatically in flavour but have the same results health wise.

I used to believe it was nuts to cook your fermented foods, thus destroying the probiotics and some of the nutrients in them. But many cultures have been doing this since they began because it actually deepens the already intense-fermented flavours and creates some beautiful, complicated and stunning dishes. Many top chefs throughout the World now are doing the same. They have whole areas of their kitchens dedicated to fermented foods and drinks, which are mostly used in their cooking.

So, in a nutshell, fermented foods and drinks are all sorts of weird, wacky, beautiful, intense, probiotic and nutrient-dense, which can be stored for prolonged periods of time for either the health benefits, taste or for later use.

Fermenting Tips

There are a few things to consider when fermenting to get the most from each batch you make and here are the ones I personally think are most important…

Sterilise

In some instances when fermenting you don't want things to be sterile as you are using the wild yeasts to super charge your fermentation. And then in other circumstances you want everything sterile as you don't want any other yeasts to interfere with the one(s) you are growing. Most of the time, however, you want something in-between. So, you want your equipment sterile and you would want to remove any mouldy parts from your vegetables, but you want to harness the bacteria on your vegetables to grow yourself some probiotics. Note: When sterilising equipment remember to do this to any weights you may be using to weigh your vegetables down.

What To Ferment In

There are so many different jars/crocks we can ferment in. Glass is great but so are purpose made clay crocks, I love both. What I would not recommend is plastic or metal. Plastic is obviously full of additional chemicals, and metal will slowly corrode from the acidity of the ferments (and some ferments simply don't like metal). Plastic is OK for a short fermenting time if BPA free and for any taps on your fermenting vessels, but other than that I would avoid them.

Organic

Where possible, and in an ideal World, what you ferment would be organic, so you are not consuming pesticides etc and so that you have the maximum number of good bacteria in your ferments. Unfortunately this is not always possible, so just do what you can where you can. Some people suggest washing your vegetables in vinegar in this instance, but as this can remove bacteria as well as other things I don't go by this rule of thumb and instead would recommend soaking them in 1 part vinegar to 9 parts water (not tap water) before using.

Less is More

Resist the urge to mess about with your ferments after you have put them in the jar. It's very tempting to want to add things in afterwards or change it in some way, but every time you do this (unless the recipe suggests it's needed) you open your jar up to contamination.

Don't Over Fill

Resist the urge to over fill your jars. Some recipes will call for filling a jar right to the top, but mostly this just becomes a messy experiment. I only ever fill jars to just below the shoulder of the jar. As the fermentation process begins, the vegetables and liquid in the jar will move up. I recommend leaving space for this to happen and putting your ferments on a tray or plate to catch any over-spill. If you over fill you will waste lots of that beautiful probiotic liquid/brine from your batch.

Burp

You'll notice many recipes call for 'burping' your jar. These are because many fermenting recipes create a lot of gas as the vegetables ferment and this gas needs to be let out. If you think you'll prefer to be a 'lazy' fermenter, then simply leave the lid on loosely instead, or when using jars with rubber around the lid you can just remove the rubber and close the lid. Nothing should be able to get in, but the gas can get out.

Discolouration

Often once the air gets to your ferments they will discolour, this is perfectly OK. You can just mix back in the top part that's discoloured and eat as normal. There is nothing wrong with your ferment and is has not gone off!

Salt

Salt is an important part of many fermented dishes. Make sure to pick a good quality salt and one that has not been tampered with like table salt. I have seen many recipes online that call for huge amounts of salt, but as a rule of thumb 1 medium cabbage should need about 1 heap tablespoon of salt. Or, if you have a set of kitchen scales, then cut up all your ingredients and weigh them, the amount of salt you add should be somewhere between 2 and 2.5% of the weight of your vegetables. This differs if you are using very watery vegetables or high sugar fruits that ferment very quickly. I have used up to 6% salt for courgette kimchi for instance as it was mainly water. A quick note on salt, if we use a good quality salt (like a sea salt for instance) then it's super good for us. Most people are salt deficient (especially if you are stressed or anxious), so don't believe the fear-mongering about salt, we need quite a lot of it!

Caffeine & Sugar

I often get asked about these being in fermented foods and drinks, as people feel they must be unhealthy then. These are added to our ferments to feed the 'starter' of the ferment, so, unless you over-fed your ferment, the ferment will eat all of the caffeine and sugar up in the fermentation process. A quick note on Kombucha: It does not need a caffeinated tea to grow, it needs the tannins from the tea instead. So, you can (as I do) make your kombucha with olive-leaf tea instead, or any other plant with tannins like raspberry or oak leaves.

Mould

Most of the time your ferments are not mouldy. And, even then, sometimes they can be saved. The thin, white, powdery stuff that you often see on olives and some other ferments is just Kham yeast and can be mixed back in, as it will do you no harm. As I mentioned earlier, sometimes ferments discolour and this may look like it's gone off, but it has not, just mix it back in. Unless you get a thick green or black mould on your ferment it's usually OK and even then, some people just scrape the top inch off and clean the edges of the jar (this happens a lot with miso) and then wait to see if it grows back, if it does not they use it, if it does then they compost it.

Make It Swim

For most ferments you want all your vegetables etc below the surface of the brine in the jar, so it doesn't become contaminated or goes off. People weigh their ferments down with many different objects, like stones (boiled), bags of water, crock weights (boiled), wax paper, plastic wrap, a cabbage leaf or a combination of a couple of the above.

Fermenting PH

Some people are worried about botulism in their ferments (or any preserving). It's highly unlikely this will occur in your ferments, but if it does worry you then there is a way to test for this. If you check the PH of your ferment when it is ready to serve it should be 4.6 or below, botulism cannot grow there.

Don't Throw It

So often I get comments, messages and emails that say that they have ruined their ferments. However, most of the time this just isn't true. As I mentioned above, sometimes your ferment will discolour or get Kham yeast on it and these are fine, in fact normal. And sometimes your ferments will turn out too salty, again this is OK. If it's too salty to enjoy then you can mix some of it with another ferment (like my cashew cream cheese, instead of adding salt) or mix it through a salad or even cook it (it won't have probiotic value anymore but will still be full of nutrients). And lastly, if it's past it's best/become to sour, or you just don't like it anymore, you can dehydrate it and use it as a probiotic seasoning, salt or stock base.

Temperature

It's always difficult to tell fermenters how long to leave their ferments, as it depends so much on the temperature of their home. In the summer months your ferments can take half as long to be ready as they do in the winter. If your home is generally quite cold, then kombucha could take up to 10 days to be ready and kraut a month. If your home is generally hot, then kombucha could be ready in 5 days and kraut 1 week. So, basically, you must experiment and allow more or less time depending on what time of the year it is. Ferments will also not keep 'good' for as long in the summer months. Usually, I use up fermented vegetables within a month in the summer if I cannot fit them in the refrigerator.

Expiry Date

When you buy shop-bought ferments they must give an expiring date, which is usually not very long. However, what I have found is that most ferments (generally not the ones with fruit in or most of the drinks) will keep for a year or more if kept cold. Just on this note too, a lot of shop-bought ferments are pasteurized (cooked) and as such have no probiotics, these ones probably have a longer expiry date and are sat on the shelves, not in the fridge, in the shop.

What I Use to Ferment

I like to use very large glass jars (between 12 & 20L jars) with plastic lids that allow the gas to escape themselves. I fill them ¾ of the way and place reusable wax sheets (like the ones used in dehydrators) that I have cut to size in the top of them. I leave my ferments for a medium of two weeks before decanting them into smaller glass jars and storing them somewhere cool.

Don't Heat them Up

When you heat fermented foods and drinks you will lose all, or at least most, of the probiotic value. You can use them in cooked foods for a deeper flavour (many top chefs now do this), but there won't be any probiotics left in them. Kimchi juice is great in omelettes and such, and it will still have a lot of nutrients in it, but the probiotics will be gone once you heat it. If you'd like to have the optimum number of probiotics, then eat it cold on the side of cooked foods instead.

Ferments Do Detox

One word of warning about fermented foods and drinks: Many people think they are allergic or intolerant to fermented foods and drinks (because they find themselves running off to the toilet after consuming them). However, for the most part, this is not the case. One of the amazing benefits of fermented foods and drinks is that they detox you. So, if you are new to them, have been on a course of anti-biotics or had a tummy bug, then you may find yourself running off to the toilet if you consume too much too soon. The reason for this is that they are detoxing you of the bad bacteria and toxins. So, start off with a small amount and slowly build up, this way they do their job but without the hidden surprises for you.

Seaweed

I love adding ground seaweed to most of my ferments. It's highly nutritious and even easier to uptake once fermented.

Animals Benefit From Fermented Foods And Drinks Too

If you have too many kefir grains or kombucha scobies, your chickens will eat them and benefit from the probiotics the same way we do. I also feed my dogs kefir grains. But the main amazing way to get your animals to benefit from fermented foods and drinks is to ferment their food too. Any dried foods can be fermented. I ferment my chicken feed (grains and seeds) for 3 days before feeding it to them. I get 3 buckets (1 for each day) of feed for them, then add water until about 2 inches above the level of the grains, and then leave it. This cuts down on food costs because there is more food, it's more nutritionally-dense, and they benefit from having probiotics each day too, keeping illnesses and diseases at bay much the same as in humans. They also eat any other fermented food that is past it's best for human consumption and love it.

How You Can Support Your Detoxing Journey

It's important to remember that when you consume probiotic (i.e., good bacteria) the bad bacteria in your system will start to leave. This means you may eliminate them through sweat, urine, bowel movements and period blood.

As I mentioned earlier in this book, many people (including myself at the beginning) believe they are intolerant or even allergic to fermented foods and drinks as it moves through them very quickly at the start, often causing very loose stools. This is your body detoxing itself of all the bad bacteria and is a good thing. Just have a little less next time and slowly build up.

It's a good idea to support yourself during this time of detoxing (which will settle down), so that it's less intense and the most effective it can be. Below are some of my top-tips for detoxing (for more information check out my book *Living A Life Less Toxic*).

1. Body-Brushing – I honestly believe everyone should be body-brushing everyday as it helps to eliminate daily toxins you take on board, and the years of built-up toxins inside you as well. Body-brushing also supports the lymphatics. I have known people who get detox symptoms from just body-brushing and not changing anything else.
2. Epsom Salt Bath – 1 cup of Epsom salts in a bath or foot bath for 20 mins helps bring magnesium in and draw toxins out.
3. Cut out gluten, soya and processed sugars from your diet wherever possible.

4. Have as many fermented foods and drinks as you can manage every day. A wide variety of them helps give you a wide variety of probiotics too.
5. Ask yourself when shopping and eating – is this nourishing or nurturing for mind, body or spirit? Become a conscious shopper and eater!
6. Consider replacing some of your cleaning products with more natural versions.
7. Consider doing the same with your skin, hair and dental products.
8. If you suffer with any sort of regular stress, anxiety or feelings of being overwhelmed, then consider staying off the stimulants (coffee, processed sugars and lots of white carbohydrates) that spike the blood sugars.
9. Listen to your body, if you feel bad after eating a certain type of food, stop eating it. If you ignore your body's messages it will only shout louder.
10. Meditate, tap, visualize or use any other mind detox methods you have in your tool belt. Being in a bad state of mind is the first step to being in a bad state of body, which can lead to choosing less-nurturing and less-nourishing options for yourself.

Sauerkrauts

Many people think Sauerkraut is from Germany when in fact, although it's been a major part of German cuisine for a long time, it came from China (where it was originally fermented with rice wine instead of salt and water). It then found its way to other Eastern European countries before settling in Germany too. It is believed that sauerkraut is one of the oldest ways to preserve vegetables and has been documented as far back as 400B.C.

Basic Sauerkraut

Ingredients

1 medium cabbage
1 tbsp. sea salt
Optional:
1 tbsp. caraway, coriander, fenugreek or fennel seeds

3 tbsp. grated ginger (I highly recommend this addition)
200-300g grated carrot (add ¼ extra tbsp. salt if adding carrots)

Directions

1. Remove outer leaves from the cabbage and set them aside.
2. Shred cabbage. I like to use the grating option of my food processor for this, but you can also cut with a knife very thinly.
3. Shred carrots and ginger (if you're adding these).
4. In a bowl, mix the shredded items with seeds (if you're adding these) and sea salt. Then massage/squeeze or pound down with a mallet, kraut pounder, the end of a rolling pin or your hands for 10 minutes.
5. Once the juices have been released, place into a wide-mouthed jar and continue to pound down until juices come up and cover the vegetables. (If this does not happen, then add a little fresh water until it covers the cabbage well.) Leave at least 2 inches at the top.
6. Place a whole cabbage leaf over the top of the vegetables (and under the juice/brine), making sure no air can get to the vegetables underneath. If you have no cabbage leaf left, then use wax paper, a boiled stone, a sterile weight of some sort or even a bag of salted water (the salt is there in case the bag splits) to weigh it all down.
7. Store away from direct sunlight, in a place not too hot or not too cold, on a plate or saucer (in case of leaks if you have overfilled) with the lid loose, or remember to burp daily. Leave for at least a week, but preferably 2 – 4 weeks.

Rainbow Sauerkraut

Ingredients

½ a small white cabbage
½ a small red cabbage
5 medium carrots, grated
1.5 tbsp. sea salt

Directions

1. Remove outer leaves from the cabbages and set them aside.
2. Shred the cabbages separately using the grating option of the food processor, or you can also cut with a knife very thinly and put cabbages into separate bowls.
3. Do the same with the carrots, adding this to its own bowl.
4. Add ½ tbsp. of salt to each of the bowls.
5. Then, for each bowl, massage/squeeze or pound down with a mallet, kraut pounder, the end of a rolling pin or your hands for 10 minutes.
6. Once the juices have been released, place the red cabbage into the bottom of a large jar and continue to pound down until juices come up and cover the vegetables. (If this does not happen, then add a little filtered water to cover).
7. Add the carrots on top, pushing down to make sure there are no air bubbles.
8. Then add the white cabbage on top and push down again.
9. Leave at least 2 inches at the top.
10. Place a whole cabbage leaf over the top of the vegetables (and under the juice/brine), making sure no air can get to the vegetables underneath. If you have no cabbage leaf left, then use wax paper, a boiled stone, a sterile weight of some sort or even a bag of salted water (the salt is there in case the bag splits) to weigh it all down.
11. Store away from direct sunlight, in a place not too hot or not too cold, on a plate or saucer (in case of leaks if you have overfilled) with the lid loose, or remember to burp daily. Leave for at least a week, but preferably 2 – 4 weeks.

Notes

› This is a lovely ferment for a gift as it looks beautiful in its jar.
› I always put the darkest ferment on the bottom and lightest on the top, so that the colours don't blend too much in the jar.
› You can use other vegetables instead, like peppers, ginger, beetroot etc.

Red Cabbage & Ginger Sauerkraut

Ingredients

1 medium red cabbage
1 tbsp. sea salt
2-4 tbsp. grated ginger

Directions

1. Remove outer leaves from the cabbage and set them aside.
2. Shred cabbage. I like to use the grating option of my food processor for this, but you can also cut with a knife very thinly.
3. In a bowl, mix the shredded items and sea salt, then massage/squeeze or pound down with a mallet, kraut pounder, the end of a rolling pin or your hands for 10 minutes.
4. Once the juices have been released, place into a wide-mouthed jar and continue to pound down until juices come up and cover the vegetables. (If this does not happen, then add a little fresh water until it covers the cabbage well.) Leave at least 2 inches at the top.
5. Place a whole cabbage leaf over the top of the vegetables (and under the juice/brine), making sure no air can get to the vegetables underneath. If you have no cabbage leaf left, then use wax paper, a boiled stone, a sterile weight of some sort or even a bag of salted water (the salt is there in case the bag splits) to weigh it all down.
6. Store away from direct sunlight, in a place not too hot or not too cold, on a plate or saucer (in case of leaks if you have overfilled) with the lid loose, or remember to burp daily. Leave for at least a week, but preferably 2 – 4 weeks.

Golden Sauerkraut

For an extra special anti-inflammatory fermenting kick...

Ingredients

1 medium white cabbage, thinly shredded or grated
2 carrots, thinly shredded or grated
5 medium garlic gloves, peeled and mashed
4-5 cm's of ginger root, peeled and diced
1-1.5 tsp. ground turmeric powder
¼ tsp. ground pepper
3 tbsp. sea salt

Directions

1. Put all the ingredients and salt (apart from the turmeric) in a large bowl, mix and set aside (covered) for about an hour so that the cabbage starts to release liquid/brine.
2. After an hour, squeeze the vegetables to release as much liquid/brine as possible.
3. Add the turmeric and mix well.
4. Once the juices have been released, place into a wide-mouthed jar and continue to pound down until juices come up and cover the vegetables. (If this does not happen, then add a little fresh water until it covers the cabbage well.) Leave at least 2 inches at the top.
5. Place a whole cabbage leaf over the top of the vegetables (and under the juice/brine), making sure no air can get to the vegetables underneath. If you have no cabbage leaf left, then use wax paper, a boiled stone, a sterile weight of some sort or even a bag of salted water (the salt is there in case the bag splits) to weigh it all down.
6. Store away from direct sunlight, in a place not too hot or not too cold, on a plate or saucer (in case of leaks if you have overfilled) with the lid loose, or remember to burp daily. Leave for at least a week, but preferably 2 – 4 weeks.

Celeriac & Ginger Sauerkraut

Ingredients

1 celeriac, peeled and chopped into quarters
2-3 cm's of fresh ginger
1 tsp. mustard or coriander seeds
2 tbsp. sea salt

Directions

1. Using the grating/shredding function on a food processor, grate the celeriac and ginger.
2. In a bowl, mix the shredded items and sea salt, then massage/squeeze or pound down with a mallet, kraut pounder, the end of a rolling pin or your hands for 10 minutes.
3. Once the juices have been released, place into a wide-mouthed jar and continue to pound down until juices come up and cover the vegetables. (If this does not happen, then add a little fresh water until it covers the cabbage well.) Leave at least 2 inches at the top.
4. Place a whole cabbage leaf over the top of the vegetables (and under the juice/brine), making sure no air can get to the vegetables underneath. If you don't have a cabbage leaf, then use wax paper, a boiled stone, a sterile weight of some sort or even a bag of salted water (the salt is there in case the bag splits) to weigh it all down.
5. Store away from direct sunlight, in a place not too hot or not too cold, on a plate or saucer (in case of leaks if you have overfilled) with the lid loose, or remember to burp daily. Leave for at least a week, but preferably 2 – 4 weeks.

Beetroot & Ginger Sauerkraut

Ingredients

4-5 large beetroot, wash, then cut off the top and tail
1/2 a small red cabbage
5-6 cm's of fresh ginger
2 tbsp. sea salt

Directions

1. Using the grating/shredding function on a food processor, grate the beetroot, cabbage and ginger.
2. In a bowl, mix the shredded items and sea salt, then massage/squeeze or pound down with a mallet, kraut pounder, the end of a rolling pin or your hands for 10 minutes.
3. Once the juices have been released, place into a wide-mouthed jar and continue to pound down until juices come up and cover the vegetables. (If this does not happen, then add a little fresh water until it covers the cabbage well.) Leave at least 2 inches at the top.
4. Place a whole cabbage leaf over the top of the vegetables (and under the juice/brine), making sure no air can get to the vegetables underneath. If you have no cabbage leaf left, then use wax paper, a boiled stone, a sterile weight of some sort or even a bag of salted water (the salt is there in case the bag splits) to weigh it all down.
5. Store away from direct sunlight, in a place not too hot or not too cold, on a plate or saucer (in case of leaks if you have overfilled) with the lid loose, or remember to burp daily. Leave for at least a week, but preferably 2 – 4 weeks.

Curried Squash Sauerkraut

Ingredients

1 small squash, de-seeded and peeled
4 large carrots
1 tsp. ginger granules or 2-3 cm's of fresh ginger
1 tsp. garlic granules or 1 clove garlic, mashed

1 tbsp. of curry powder
1 tsp. cumin seeds
1 tsp. mustard seeds
3 tbsp. sea salt

Directions

1. Using the grating/shredding function in the food processor, grate the squash, carrots and ginger.
2. In a bowl, mix the shredded items, all the other ingredients and sea salt, then massage/squeeze or pound down with a mallet, kraut pounder, the end of a rolling pin or your hands for 10 minutes.
3. Once the juices have been released, place into a wide-mouthed jar and continue to pound down until juices come up and cover the vegetables. (If this does not happen, then add a little fresh water until it covers the cabbage well.) Leave at least 2 inches at the top.
4. Place a whole cabbage leaf over the top of the vegetables (and under the juice/brine), making sure no air can get to the vegetables underneath. If you have no cabbage leaf left, then use wax paper, a boiled stone, a sterile weight of some sort or even a bag of salted water (the salt is there in case the bag splits) to weigh it all down.
5. Store away from direct sunlight, in a place not too hot or not too cold, on a plate or saucer (in case of leaks if you have overfilled) with the lid loose, or remember to burp daily. Leave for at least a week, but preferably 2 – 4 weeks.

Courgette & Turmeric Sauerkraut

Ingredients

2-3 large courgettes
1 small red onion
3-4 cm's of fresh ginger
2 garlic gloves or 1 tsp. garlic granules
1/2 paprika granules

1/4 tsp. turmeric granules
3 tbsp. sea salt

Directions

1. Using the grating/shredding function on a food processor, grate the courgette, onion, ginger and garlic and add to a large bowl with all of the other ingredients, including the sea salt.
2. Mix the items and sea salt, then massage/squeeze or pound down with a mallet, kraut pounder, the end of a rolling pin or your hands for 10 minutes.
3. Once the juices have been released, place into a wide-mouthed jar and continue to pound down until juices come up and cover the vegetables. (If this does not happen, then add a little fresh water until it covers the cabbage well.) Leave at least 2 inches at the top.
4. Place a whole cabbage leaf over the top of the vegetables (and under the juice/brine), making sure no air can get to the vegetables underneath. If you have no cabbage leaf left, then use wax paper, a boiled stone, a sterile weight of some sort or even a bag of salted water (the salt is there in case the bag splits) to weigh it all down.
5. Store away from direct sunlight, in a place not too hot or not too cold, on a plate or saucer (in case of leaks if you have overfilled) with the lid loose, or remember to burp daily. Leave for 3 days and consume before 1 month (courgette-based ferments often turn to a baby-food consistency after this time period, unless you add much more salt).

Christmas Sauerkraut

Ingredients

1/2 large white cabbage
3 apples
2 tsp. cloves
1 tsp. cinnamon
1/2 tsp. nutmeg
1/2 tsp. mixed spice

1 tsp. of sea salt
Optional: Handful of raisins and slices of orange placed around the inside of the jar as you start to fill it

Directions

1. Using a food processor on the shredding/grating function grate the cabbage and apples. Save the outer leaf of the cabbage.
2. In a bowl, mix the shredded items and sea salt, then massage/squeeze or pound down with a mallet, kraut pounder, the end of a rolling pin or your hands for 10 minutes.
3. Once the juices have been released, place into a wide-mouthed jar and continue to pound down until juices come up and cover the vegetables. (If this does not happen, then add a little fresh water until it covers the cabbage well.) Leave at least 2 inches at the top.
4. Place a whole cabbage leaf over the top of the vegetables (and under the juice/brine), making sure no air can get to the vegetables underneath. If you have no cabbage leaf left, then use wax paper, a boiled stone, a sterile weight of some sort or even a bag of salted water (the salt is there in case the bag splits) to weigh it all down.
5. Store away from direct sunlight, in a place not too hot or not too cold, on a plate or saucer (in case of leaks if you have overfilled) with the lid loose, or remember to burp daily. Leave for at least a week, but preferably 2 – 4 weeks.

Notes

Fruit ferments won't keep as long as other ferments, because of the higher sugar content which leads to the mixture continuing to ferment.

Indian Sauerkraut

Ingredients

1 small white cabbage (or a red one for a change)
1 small yellow onion
3 garlic cloves
4 cm's of ginger, peeled
1/2 tsp. cumin seeds

1 tbsp. sea salt

1/2 tsp. mustard seeds
1/2 tsp. coriander seeds
1/2 tsp. fennel seeds
1/2 tsp. black peppercorns
1/2 tsp. turmeric powder
1 tsp. curry powder

Directions

1. Put cabbage, carrots, onion, garlic and ginger in a food processor using the grating/shredding function or thinly slice by hand.
2. In a bowl, mix the shredded items, plus everything else, then massage/squeeze or pound down with a mallet, kraut pounder, the end of a rolling pin or your hands for 10 minutes.
3. Once the juices have been released, place into a wide-mouthed jar and continue to pound down until juices come up and cover the vegetables. (If this does not happen, then add a little fresh water until it covers the cabbage well.) Leave at least 2 inches at the top.
4. Place a whole cabbage leaf over the top of the vegetables (and under the juice/brine), making sure no air can get to the vegetables underneath. If you have no cabbage leaf left, then use wax paper, a boiled stone, a sterile weight of some sort or even a bag of salted water (the salt is there in case the bag splits) to weigh it all down.
5. Store away from direct sunlight, in a place not too hot or not too cold, on a plate or saucer (in case of leaks if you have overfilled) with the lid loose, or remember to burp daily. Leave for at least a week, but preferably 2 – 4 weeks.

Nettle, Garlic & Fenugreek Sauerkraut

Ingredients

1 medium white cabbage, finely sliced
3-4 garlic cloves, peeled and chopped finely
1 tsp. fenugreek powder
1 tsp. seaweed flakes (optional)
1/2 – 1 tsp. ginger powder (optional)
1 tsp. sea salt

4-5 handfuls of nettles leaves (just the tops), washed (If nettles not available, I use either the petals of marigolds or 1 tsp. of caraway seeds instead. If not using nettles, don't add the garlic either)

Directions

1. Put the cabbage through a food processor using the grating/shredding function or thinly slice by hand.
2. Rinse and chop the nettles (put gloves on if they bother you).
3. Put all the ingredients in a bowl, mix well and start squeezing/massaging or pounding with a mallet, kraut pounder, the end of a rolling pin or your hands for 10 minutes to release all the liquid from the ingredients.
4. Once the juices have been released, place into a wide-mouthed jar and continue to pound down until juices come up and cover the vegetables. (If this does not happen, then add a little fresh water until it covers the cabbage well.) Leave at least 2 inches at the top.
5. Place a whole cabbage leaf over the top of the vegetables (and under the juice/brine), making sure no air can get to the vegetables underneath. If you have no cabbage leaf left, then use wax paper, a boiled stone, a sterile weight of some sort or even a bag of salted water (the salt is there in case the bag splits) to weigh it all down.
6. Store away from direct sunlight, in a place not too hot or not too cold, on a plate or saucer (in case of leaks if you have overfilled) with the lid loose, or remember to burp daily. Leave for at least a week, but preferably 2 – 4 weeks.

Curtido

A typical Central American fermented relish usually served with stuffed pupusas. The Curtido is thought to be traced to a 10,000-year old Egyptian vase, and is even talked about in the Bible.

Ingredients

1 medium white cabbage, thinly cut or grated
1 medium white onion, chopped
2 medium carrots, grated
2 jalapeno peppers, diced small
2 tbsp. fresh oregano, or 1 tbsp. of dried
1.5 tbsp. sea salt
Juice of half a lime (optional)

Directions

1. Put all the Ingredients into a large bowl and mix.
2. Squeeze (or pound down with a kraut pounder) the mixture until liquid/brine starts to come out of the vegetables.
3. Once the juices have been released, place into a wide-mouthed jar and continue to pound down until juices come up and cover the vegetables. (If this does not happen, then add a little fresh water until it covers the cabbage well.) Leave at least 2 inches at the top.
4. Place a whole cabbage leaf over the top of the vegetables (and under the juice/brine), making sure no air can get to the vegetables underneath. If you have no cabbage leaf left, then use wax paper, a boiled stone, a sterile weight of some sort or even a bag of salted water (the salt is there in case the bag splits) to weigh it all down.
5. Store away from direct sunlight, in a place not too hot or not too cold, on a plate or saucer (in case of leaks if you have overfilled) with the lid loose, or remember to burp daily. Leave for at least a week, but preferably 2 – 4 weeks.

Kimchi

There is no doubt where Kimchi came from and that is Korea. It's thought to date back to 57 B.C. It originally wasn't spicy and had a base of radish instead of cabbage, which seems to be the norm these days.

Basic Kimchi

Ingredients

1 medium green cabbage or Chinese cabbage, shredded
1 bunch green onions or 1 small white or red onion, sliced thinly
1 large carrot, grated
3 cloves, minced
3cm of fresh ginger, minced
½ a red pepper, sliced thinly
1 inch of fresh horseradish minced (or 2 or 3 of any other spicy radishes sliced)
½ to 1 tsp. of chili flakes (or powder)
1 ½ tbsp. sea salt
1 tsp. fish sauce or half 1 tsp. of seaweed flakes (optional)

Directions

1. Place cabbage into a bowl with the salt and squeeze (or pound down with a kraut pounder) the mixture until liquid/brine starts to come out of the vegetables. It's easier to leave the bowl covered with the ingredients for a few hours and come back to this. Get as much liquid out of the cabbage as possible because this will form your brine.
2. Add all the other ingredients to the bowl and mix well.
3. Place into a wide-mouthed jar and continue to pound down until juices come up and cover the vegetables. (If this does not happen, then add a little fresh water until it covers the cabbage well.) Leave at least 2 inches at the top.
4. Place a whole cabbage leaf over the top of the vegetables (and under the juice/brine), making sure no air can get to the vegetables underneath. If you have no cabbage leaf left, then use wax paper, a boiled stone, a sterile weight of some sort or even a bag of salted water (the salt is there in case the bag splits) to weigh it all down.
5. Store away from direct sunlight, in a place not too hot or not too cold, on a plate or saucer (in case of leaks if you have overfilled) with the lid loose, or remember to burp daily. Leave for at least a week, but preferably 2 – 4 weeks.

Notes

› You can put the ginger, garlic and chili through a food processor with a little water and add this to the kimchi as a paste, this works well and is my preferred method.
› You can add any seasonal vegetables or even flowers to your kimchi. Beetroot kimchi is truly amazing, I add 1 beetroot per cabbage. Marigold or rose petals are also a wonderful addition to Kimchis, and even elderflowers too.

Golden or Curried Kimchi

Ingredients

1 medium green cabbage or Chinese cabbage, shredded

1 bunch green onions or 1 small white or red onion, sliced thinly

1 large carrot, grated

3 garlic cloves, minced

3 cm's of fresh ginger, minced

½ a red pepper, sliced thinly

1 inch of fresh horseradish, minced (or 2 or 3 of any other spicy radishes sliced)

1 tsp. of turmeric powder (for Golden Kraut)

1-1 ½ tsp. of powdered Garam Masala (for Curried Kimchi – I also like to add the same amount of chili powder too for some heat)

1 ½ tbsp. sea salt

1 tsp. fish sauce or half 1 tsp. of seaweed flakes (optional)

Directions

1. Place cabbage into a bowl with the salt and squeeze (or pound down with a kraut pounder) the mixture until liquid/brine starts to come out of the vegetables. It's easier to leave the bowl covered with the ingredients for a few hours and come back to this. Get as much liquid out of the cabbage as possible as this will form your brine.
2. Add all the other ingredients to the bowl and mix well.
3. Place into a wide-mouthed jar and continue to pound down until juices come up and cover the vegetables. (If this does not happen, then add a little fresh water until it covers the cabbage well.) Leave at least 2 inches at the top of space.
4. Place a whole cabbage leaf over the top of the vegetables (and under the juice/brine), making sure no air can get to the vegetables underneath. If you have no cabbage leaf left, then use wax paper, a boiled stone, a sterile weight of some sort or even a bag of salted water (the salt is there in case the bag splits) to weigh it all down.
5. Store away from direct sunlight, in a place not too hot or not too cold, on a plate or saucer (in case of leaks if you have overfilled) with the lid loose, or remember to burp daily. Leave for at least a week, but preferably 2 – 4 weeks.

Notes

› You can put the ginger, garlic and chili through a food processor with a little water and add this to the kimchi as a paste, this works well and is my preferred method.

Miso Kimchi

Ingredients

1/2 a large cabbage, chopped into inch squares
1 red pepper, chopped into inch squares
1 yellow pepper, chopped into inch squares
1 bag of radish, sliced
1 bunch of spring onions, chopped
2 leaks, cut length-ways and then chopped
2 inches of ginger, grated
2 garlic cloves, grated

4-6 tbsp. of chili powder or flakes (more if you prefer it hotter)
4 tbsp. of miso paste
3 tsp. of sea salt
2 tbsp. of seaweed flakes (optional, but in my mind highly desirable for taste and nutrient content)

Directions

1. Put the cabbage and salt into a large bowl and mix well. Then squeeze or pound the cabbage until the juices come out. Then add all the other ingredients and mix well.
2. Once the juices have been released, place into a wide-mouthed jar and continue to pound down until juices come up and cover the vegetables. (If this does not happen, then add a little fresh water until it covers the cabbage well.) Leave at least 2 inches at the top.
3. Place a whole cabbage leaf over the top of the vegetables (and under the juice/brine), making sure no air can get to the vegetables underneath. If you have no cabbage leaf left, then use wax paper, a boiled stone, a sterile weight of some sort or even a bag of salted water (the salt is there in case the bag splits) to weigh it all down.
4. Store away from direct sunlight, in a place not too hot or not too cold, on a plate or saucer (in case of leaks if you have overfilled) with the lid loose, or remember to burp daily. Leave for at least a week, but preferably 2 – 4 weeks.

Kimchi Kraut

Ingredients

1/2 head white cabbage
2 carrots (parsnips also work well)
7-8 red radishes
1 small celeriac (optional)
1 small yellow onion
2 inch square fresh ginger

4 cloves garlic (optional)
1 tsp. dried chili flakes
1 tbsp. sea salt
25-50ml filtered water or sauerkraut juice

Directions

1. Using the shredding/grating function on your food processor, or a hand grater, grate all the vegetables.
2. In a bowl, mix the shredded items and everything else, then massage/squeeze or pound down with a mallet, kraut pounder, the end of a rolling pin or your hands for 10 minutes.
3. Once the juices have been released, place into a wide-mouthed jar and continue to pound down until juices come up and cover the vegetables. (If this does not happen, then add a little fresh water until it covers the cabbage well.) Leave at least 2 inches at the top.
4. Place a whole cabbage leaf over the top of the vegetables (and under the juice/brine), making sure no air can get to the vegetables underneath. If you have no cabbage leaf, then use wax paper or a sterile weight of some sort to weigh it down.
5. Store away from direct sunlight, in a place not too hot or not too cold (like the kids story) on a plate or saucer (in case of leaks if you have overfilled) with the lid loose, or remember to burp daily. Leave for at least a week, but preferably 2 – 4 weeks.

Notes

› You can use just about any vegetables in this recipe, so it's a great way to use up veggies!

Carrot Kimchi

Ingredients

3-4 carrots
2-3 cm's of fresh ginger
3-4 garlic cloves, sliced
1 tsp. miso paste
2 tbsp. sesame seed oil
2 tbsp of dried seaweed

1 tsp. chili powder
1 tsp. chili flakes
1 tsp. black pepper, freshly ground
1 tsp. sea salt

Directions

1. Using the grating/shredding function on a food processor, grate the carrot, garlic and ginger and add to a large bowl with the other ingredients, except the chili powder and flakes.
2. Mix the shredded items and then massage/squeeze or pound down with a mallet, kraut pounder, the end of a rolling pin or your hands for 10 minutes. Then add in the chili powder and flakes and mix well.
3. Once the juices have been released, place into a wide-mouthed jar and continue to pound down until juices come up and cover the vegetables. (If this does not happen, then add a little fresh water until it covers the cabbage well.) Leave at least 2 inches at the top.
4. Place a whole cabbage leaf over the top of the vegetables (and under the juice/brine), making sure no air can get to the vegetables underneath. If you have no cabbage leaf, then use wax paper or a sterile weight of some sort to weigh it down.
5. Store away from direct sunlight, in a place not too hot or not too cold (like the kids story) on a plate or saucer (in case of leaks if you have overfilled) with the lid loose, or remember to burp daily. Leave for at least a week, but preferably 2 – 4 weeks.

Chunky Carrot & Radish Kimchi

Ingredients

2 carrots, thinly sliced
1 bunch of radishes, topped, tailed and quartered
1/2 a bunch of spring onions, chopped
2-3 cm's of fresh ginger, thinly sliced
3-4 garlic cloves, thinly sliced
2 tbsp. sesame seed oil

2 tbsp. of dried seaweed
1 tsp. chili powder
1 tsp. black pepper, freshly ground
1 tsp. sea salt

Directions

1. Put all the ingredients in a bowl and mix well.
2. Place into a medium jar and pack down, then fill with filtered water to cover.
3. Leave at least 2 inches at the top.
4. Place a whole cabbage leaf over the top of the vegetables (and under the juice/brine), making sure no air can get to the vegetables underneath. If you have no cabbage leaf, then use wax paper or a sterile weight of some sort to weigh it down.
5. Store away from direct sunlight, in a place not too hot or not too cold (like the kids story) on a plate or saucer (in case of leaks if you have overfilled) with the lid loose, or remember to burp daily. Leave for at least a week, but preferably 2 – 4 weeks.

Un-spiced Kimchi

Ingredients

1/2 a large cabbage, chopped into inch squares
1 red pepper, chopped into inch squares
1 yellow pepper, chopped into inch squares
1 bag of radish, sliced
1 bunch of spring onions (or one small red onion), chopped

2 inches of ginger, grated
2 garlic cloves, grated
1-2 tsp. of miso paste
2 tsp. dried rosemary
3 tsp. sea salt
1 tbsp. of seaweed flakes (optional)

Directions

1. Add all ingredients to a large bowl and mix well (you will need to mush the miso in with the back of a spoon)
2. Cover and leave for 30 mins
3. Stir well, cover and leave for another 30 mins
4. Stir well one last time, cover and leave for another 30 mins
5. Add all the ingredients to a large jar
6. Pack down tightly and add a little fresh water to fill up any air gaps
7. Place into a wide-mouthed jar and continue to pound down until juices come up and cover the vegetables. Leave at least 2 inches at the top with nothing in.
8. Place a whole cabbage leaf over the top of the vegetables (and under the juice/brine), making sure no air can get to the vegetables underneath. If you have no cabbage leaf, then use wax paper or a sterile weight of some sort to weigh it down.
9. Store away from direct sunlight, in a place not too hot or not too cold (like the kids story) on a plate or saucer (in case of leaks if you have overfilled) with the lid loose, or remember to burp daily. Leave for 5 – 10 days.

Veggies

Piccalilli

Ingredients

1 white cabbage, thinly sliced
1 cauliflower, chopped up into small pieces
5 medium carrots, diced
1 bunch of spring onions, chopped including all the green, or 1 normal small onion, diced
1 red pepper, diced

Half a red chili, de-seeded and chopped fine, or 1/2 tsp. of chili powder
2 tsp. of mustard seeds
2 or 3 turmeric roots, grated, or 1 tsp. of powdered turmeric
3 tbsp. of sea salt

Directions

1. Mix the cabbage and the salt, massage until water releases from the cabbage to form a brine.
2. Add all the other ingredients to the bowl and mix well.
3. Place into a wide-mouthed jar or crock and push everything down so there are no air bubbles.
4. If there is not enough juice to come up and cover the vegetables, then add a little filtered water until it does. Leave at least 2 inches at the top with nothing in.
5. Place a whole cabbage leaf over the top of the vegetables (and under the juice/brine), making sure no air can get to the vegetables underneath. If you have no cabbage leaf left, then use wax paper, a boiled stone, a sterile weight of some sort or even a bag of salted water (the salt is there in case the bag splits) to weigh it all down.
6. Store away from direct sunlight, in a place not too hot or not too cold, on a plate or saucer (in case of leaks if you have overfilled) with the lid loose, or remember to burp daily. Leave for at least a week, but preferably 2 – 4 weeks.

Pickles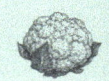

Cleopatra and Julius Caesar are both thought to have sworn by the health benefits of pickles, more than 4000 years ago. And seafarers for a long time believed pickles made them more resilient and prevented scurvy on their long voyages.

Ingredients

1 large carrot, cut into slices
1 red pepper, cut into slices
Half a small cauliflower, cut into half florets
1 clove garlic, crushed and peeled
1 bay leaf
½ tsp. coriander seeds

¼ tsp. black peppercorns
3 tsp. sea salt
Filtered water to cover
1-2 grape/raspberry/olive/vine leaves
(optional, to keep veggies crisp)

Directions

1. Place all the ingredients apart from the water and salt in a large mason jar.
2. Make sure there is at least 2 inches of space in the top of the jar.
3. Add the salt and then the water to cover all the vegetables.
4. Place a whole cabbage leaf over the top of the vegetables (and under the juice/brine), making sure no air can get to the vegetables underneath. If you have no cabbage leaves, then use wax paper or a sterile weight of some sort to weigh it down.
5. Store away from direct sunlight, in a place not too hot or not too cold (like the kids story) on a plate or saucer (in case of leaks if you have overfilled) with the lid loose, or remember to burp daily.
6. This is ready to eat after 5 days but will keep for many weeks, especially if you add the grape/raspberry leaves.
7. Do not eat the grape/raspberry/olive/vine leaves.

Curried Cauliflower

Ingredients

1 cauliflower, cut into small pieces
½ an onion, chopped finely
6-8 garlic cloves, smashed
4-6 small dried chilis, chopped
2 tbsp. curry powder
1 tbsp. chili powder
1 tbsp. turmeric powder
1 tsp. cayenne
2-4 tbsp. of kombucha, kimchi or kraut juice
Filtered water to top up
2 tbsp. sea salt

Directions

1. Rinse and cut the cauliflower into small pieces.
2. Put all the ingredients into a bowl and mix well.
3. Place into a wide-mouthed jar and add water to cover.
4. Leave at least 2 inches at the top.
5. Place a whole cabbage leaf over the top of the vegetables (and under the juice/brine), making sure no air can get to the vegetables underneath. If you have no cabbage leaf left, then use wax paper, a boiled stone, a sterile weight of some sort or even a bag of salted water (the salt is there in case the bag splits) to weigh it all down.
6. Store away from direct sunlight, in a place not too hot or not too cold, on a plate or saucer (in case of leaks if you have overfilled) with the lid loose, or remember to burp daily. Leave for at least 7 – 10 days.

Peppers

Ingredients

2-3 peppers, cored and cut into strips
1 small handful of parsley
1 small garlic clove, peeled
1 tsp. Himalayan or sea salt
Filtered water to cover

Directions

1. Add the parsley and garlic to a mason jar.
2. Place the peppers in the jar so that they are all standing up right in the jar. Make sure there are enough peppers so that they are wedged in and won't move anywhere when the liquid is added.
3. Add the salt and then fill with the water until the peppers are completely covered. Make sure there is a space of at least 2 inches between the water and the top of the jar.
4. Place a whole cabbage leaf over the top of the vegetables (and under the juice/brine), making sure no air can get to the vegetables underneath. If you have no cabbage leaf, then use wax paper or a sterile weight of some sort to weigh it down.
5. Store away from direct sunlight, in a place not too hot or not too cold (like the kids story), on a plate or saucer (in case of leaks if you have overfilled) with the lid loose, or remember to burp daily.
6. These are fine to eat after 5 days or up to a few weeks old.

'Pickled' Onions

Ingredients

300-400g of small shallots/pickling onions, peeled
A small handful of fresh rosemary, parsley or cumin seeds
1 tbsp. sea salt
Filtered water to cover

Directions

1. Place any herbs you wish to add into a large jar.
2. Add the salt and then the onions.
3. Fill the jar with water, so that all the onions are covered.
4. Place a whole cabbage leaf over the top of the vegetables (and under the juice/brine), making sure no air can get to the vegetables underneath. If you have no cabbage leaf, then use wax paper or a sterile weight of some sort to weigh it down.
5. Place some muslin over the top of the jar and secure it in place with an elastic band.
6. Store away from direct sunlight, in a place not too hot or not too cold (like the kids story), on a plate or saucer (in case of leaks if you have overfilled).
7. These are ready to eat after 2 weeks or for months beyond this.
8. Once you start to eat from the jar, put a lid on it and place in the fridge.

Carrot and Garlic Sticks

Ingredients

5-6 carrots, washed and cut into sticks about 4 inches long
2-3 garlic cloves, peeled
A small handful of fresh dill (optional)
2 tsp. sea salt
Filtered water to cover

Directions

1. Add the dill (if using), garlic and salt to a large jar.
2. Wedge the carrot sticks into the jar so that they are all standing up and cannot move or float around once you add the liquid.
3. Add the water and make sure the sticks are fully covered, but that there is still a 2 inch space between the water and the top of the jar.
4. Place a whole cabbage leaf over the top of the vegetables (and under the juice/brine), making sure no air can get to the vegetables underneath. If you have no cabbage leaf, then use wax paper or a sterile weight of some sort to weigh it down.
5. Store away from direct sunlight, in a place not too hot or not too cold (like the kids story), on a plate or saucer (in case of leaks if you have overfilled) with the lid loose, or remember to burp daily.
6. These are ready to eat in 5 days or for up to a month.
7. Once you start eating from the jar, place the jar in the fridge.

Parsnip & Carrot Sticks

Ingredients

1-2 parsnips (depending on size), topped and tailed, peeled and cut into 4 inch sticks
1-2 carrots, cut into 4 inch sticks
2 inches of fresh ginger, peeled and sliced
1 tbsp. chili flakes
1 tsp. sea salt
Filtered water to cover

Directions

1. Place ginger, chili flakes and salt into a large jar.
2. Place the parsnip and carrot sticks into the jar so they are all standing up on their ends. Wedge them in as tightly as you can so that none of the vegetable sticks can float about once you add the liquid.
3. Add the water to cover the stick fully, but make sure there is also a 2 inch space between the top of the water and the top of the jar.
4. Place a whole cabbage leaf over the top of the vegetables (and under the juice/brine), making sure no air can get to the vegetables underneath. If you have no cabbage leaf, then use wax paper or a sterile weight of some sort to weigh it down.
5. Store away from direct sunlight, in a place not too hot or not too cold (like the kids story), on a plate or saucer (in case of leaks if you have overfilled) with the lid loose, or remember to burp daily.
6. These sticks are ready to eat after 5 days or for up to a month.
7. Once you start eating from the jar place it in the fridge.

Salsa

Ingredients

6 tomatoes, chopped
2 red onions, chopped
3 red, yellow and/or green peppers, chopped
4-5 spring onions, chopped
2-3 medium chilies, finely sliced
3 garlic cloves, minced

1-2 limes, just the juice
1 tsp. cayenne pepper, ground
1 tsp. paprika, ground
2 tbsp. sea salt

Directions

1. Place everything in a large jar and squash it all down.
2. Add filtered water to cover the vegetables.
3. Make sure everything is below the level of the water.
4. Make sure there is at least 2 cm's of space in the top of the jar.
5. Place a whole cabbage leaf over the top of the vegetables (and under the juice/brine), making sure no air can get to the vegetables underneath. If you have no cabbage leaf, then use wax paper or a sterile weight of some sort to weigh it down.
6. Store away from direct sunlight, in a place not too hot or not too cold (like the kids story), on a plate or saucer (in case of leaks if you have overfilled) with the lid loose, or remember to burp daily. Leave for 3–5 days.
7. Once you start consuming from the jar, put it in the fridge.

Pineapple & Papaya Salsa

Ingredients

1 small pineapple, peeled and chopped into small pieces

2 papayas, peeled, de-seeded and chopped into small pieces

1 medium red onion, peeled and chopped into small pieces

1 large pepper (colour of your choosing), de-seeded and chopped into small pieces

4-6 inches of fresh ginger, peeled and diced or grated into tiny pieces

1-3 fresh chilies (depending how hot you like it), cut into very small pieces

1 bunch of parsley, finely chopped

1-2 tsp. of garlic granules

1-2 tbsp. sauerkraut or kimchi juice (that has already fermented)

2 tbsp. sea salt

1-2 tsp. chili powder (optional)

Directions

1. Add all the ingredients to a large bowl and mix well.
2. Place into two medium jars and pack down, then fill with filtered water.
3. Make sure everything is below the level of the water.
4. Place a whole cabbage leaf over the top of the vegetables (and under the juice/brine), making sure no air can get to the vegetables underneath. If you have no cabbage leaf, then use wax paper, a boiled stone, a sterile weight of some sort or even a bag of salted water (the salt is there in case the bag splits) to weigh it all down.
5. Store away from direct sunlight, in a place not too hot or not too cold, on a plate or saucer (in case of leaks if you have overfilled) with the lid loose, or remember to burp daily.
6. This is ready after 3 days, but I prefer to leave it 5 days for extra probiotic-ness. Once you start consuming from the jar, put it in the fridge.

Garlic Mushrooms

Ingredients

A selection of your favourite mushrooms to fill a jar of your choice, sliced thinly
5-6 garlic cloves, sliced
2 tbsp. of kombucha, kimchi or kraut juice
1 tsp. cayenne pepper
1 tsp. dried oregano (or coriander if you prefer)
1 tsp. black pepper
1 tsp. sea salt

Directions

1. Place all the ingredients, except the mushrooms, into your jar.
2. Pack the mushrooms in on top of everything else.
3. Add filtered water to cover the mushrooms.
4. Make sure everything is below the level of the water.
5. Leave at least 2 inches of space at the top.
6. Place a whole cabbage leaf over the top of the vegetables (and under the juice/brine), making sure no air can get to the vegetables underneath. If you don't have a cabbage leaf, then use wax paper, a boiled stone, a sterile weight of some sort or even a bag of salted water (the salt is there in case the bag splits) to weigh it all down.
7. Store away from direct sunlight, in a place not too hot or not too cold, on a plate or saucer (in case of leaks if you have overfilled) with the lid loose, or remember to burp daily. Leave for 3–5 days.
8. Once you start consuming from the jar, put it in the fridge.

Onion Relish

Ingredients

3 or 4 large onions, peeled and sliced thinly or grated
1-2 tbsp. peppercorns
2 tsp. sea salt
Filtered water to cover

Directions

1. Place all the ingredients in a large bowl and mix well.
2. Leave covered for 30 minutes, until some of the liquid from the onions has started to collect in the bowl.
3. Place everything (including the liquid) into a large jar and press down so that the liquid comes up above the onions. Add a little filtered water if this does not happen.
4. Place a whole cabbage leaf over the top of the vegetables (and under the juice/brine), making sure no air can get to the vegetables underneath. If you have no cabbage leaf, then use wax paper, a boiled stone, a sterile weight of some sort or even a bag of salted water (the salt is there in case the bag splits) to weigh it all down.
5. Store away from direct sunlight, in a place not too hot or not too cold, on a plate or saucer (in case of leaks if you have overfilled) with the lid loose, or remember to burp daily.
6. The relish is ready to eat after a week and lasts for many months thereafter.

Spicy Fermented Aubergine Dip

Ingredients

1 large aubergine
4-6 garlic cloves, diced
1 tsp. chili flakes
1/2 tsp. paprika
1-2 tsp. dried basil
1-2 tsp. dried coriander

1/2 tsp. pepper, freshly ground
1/2 tsp. sea salt (for a medium aubergine)
Optional: 6-8 sun-dried tomatoes (in oil), chopped

Directions

1. Cut the aubergine up into small squares and add to a large bowl with the salt, mix well.
2. Leave to sit for an hour or two (stir halfway through) with some muslin or a tea-towel over the top.
3. Place all the other ingredients in the bowl with the aubergine and mix well. If it is not all mushy, then use a fork to mush it all down into more of a dip consistency.
4. Pack it all down into a jar (including the liquid from inside the aubergine). If the liquid does not come above the aubergine, mix then add a little filtered water until it does.
5. Make sure there is at least 2 cm's of space in the top of the jar and then put the lid on loosely. Use wax paper, a boiled stone, a sterile weight of some sort or even a bag of salted water (the salt is there in case the bag splits) to weight it all down.
6. Store away from direct sunlight, in a place not too hot or not too cold, on a plate or saucer (in case of leaks if you have overfilled) with the lid loose, or remember to burp daily. Leave for at least a week, but preferably 2.
7. Once you start consuming from the jar, put it in the fridge.

Tomato, Basil and Garlic

Ingredients

Enough cherry tomatoes to fill the jar of your choosing
1 large handful of fresh basil leaves
4-6 cloves of fresh garlic, thinly sliced
1 tsp. sea salt

Fresh filtered water to fill jar, and/or juice of kimchi (if you want it spicy - I like half and half) or sauerkraut juice

Directions

1. Pierce the tomatoes with a knife and add the first layer of them into your jar.
2. Add some of the basil and garlic and salt.
3. Add more tomatoes and then more basil, garlic and salt.
4. Continue until all of the tomatoes are in the jar (making sure to wedge them in so they do not float around when they are below the water).
5. Fill with water or kimchi or sauerkraut juice until just above the level of the tomatoes.
6. Place a whole cabbage leaf over the top of the vegetables (and under the juice/brine), making sure no air can get to the vegetables underneath. If you have no cabbage leaf, then use wax paper, a boiled stone, a sterile weight of some sort or even a bag of salted water (the salt is there in case the bag splits) to weigh it all down.
7. Store away from direct sunlight, in a place not too hot or not too cold, on a plate or saucer (in case of leaks if you have overfilled) with the lid loose, or remember to burp daily. Leave for 5 days.
8. Once you start consuming from the jar, put it in the fridge.

Extras

Sourdough

Sourdough dates back to Egyptian times at least, where they were using, what we call now, wild yeasts to ferment/rise the bread before baking. It's clear that Europeans then went on to use the foam of the beer to make bread (and some people still do to this day). With the invention of commercial yeasts, sourdough faded out in many places in favour of a quicker and easier bread. However, it's been making a comeback for some time now, due to that fact that it's much easier to digest and that the fermenting process often removes much of the gluten, which many people have issues with now.

Ingredients

480g flour (I prefer spelt flour)
100g sourdough starter

220ml fresh water
1 tsp. salt

Directions

1. Mix well together the 100g of sourdough starter with the 300g of flour and the 220ml of water in a bowl, and cover for 8-10 hours (at this, or any of the later stages, you can add herbs, chillies, sun-dried tomatoes or other similar items).
2. Add the remaining 180g of flour and the sugar, and knead well. Cover and allow to rest for another 2-3 hours.
3. Knead again and pop into a lightly oiled bread tin or proof basket, cover and leave in a warm place for 1-2 hours. (You can lightly score the top of the dough at this stage if you want to.)
4. Preheat your oven on a medium heat (around 350°F/180°C/gas mark 4) and place a bowl of boiling water on the bottom of your oven.
5. Place the dough in a baking tin/baking basket in the upper oven and bake for 30-35 minutes.
6. Remove from the tin and allow it to cool slightly before cutting into it.

Notes
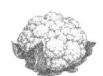

› It's super easy to make a sourdough starter and there are lots of different recipes you can find online, depending on which flour you wish to use.
› Your sourdough starter needs to be fed once a week and should live in your fridge until the day before you want to use it.
› To feed your sourdough starter, add 50g flour and 50ml fresh water. Mix well and pop back in the fridge until you want to use it.
› Your starter will separate (with the hooch lying on top). This is fine and it just needs stirring back in each week when you feed it.
› You can use sourdough instead of normal flour in many baking recipes for a lighter dough (great for heavy gluten-free recipes).
› Sourdough is no longer probiotic because it's been cooked.

Cashew 'Cheese'

Ingredients

300g cashews, soaked overnight
1 bunch of chives, chopped thinly
1 garlic clove, minced, or 1/2 tsp. of garlic granules
1/2 tsp. pepper, freshly ground
Juice of 1 lemon
2 tbsp. of fresh (a week- or two-old at most) sauerkraut or kimchi (if you want a little spice) juice
1 tsp. raw apple cider vinegar
50-100ml of filtered water (start with 50 and add a little at a time until it's a little runny)
1 tsp. of sea salt

Directions

1. Rinse off soaked cashews.
2. Place all the ingredients, apart from the chives, into a food processor and blend well.
3. If the mixture isn't a bit runny yet (but not watery), then add a little more water until it is runny.
4. Place the mixture in a bowl (much bigger than the ingredients as it expands a lot), add the chives and mix well.
5. Cover the bowl with a tea-towel or muslin and an elastic band, and leave on the kitchen side overnight or until it starts to expand.
6. Place into a medium sized jar and leave in the fridge for up to two weeks.

Pumpkin Seed 'Cheese'

Ingredients

200g pumpkin seeds (soaked for 3 days and rinsed well – note that the seeds smell kind of bad at this stage)
1 small onion, finely chopped
2 tsp. seaweed flakes
2 garlic cloves, finely chopped
3 tbsp. nutritional yeast
2 tsp. miso paste
1 tbsp. turmeric
1 tsp. cayenne pepper
½ tsp. of good quality salt
2 tbsp. olive oil
100-150 ml water to blend
50ml of kombucha, kimchi or kraut juice (optional)

Directions

1. In a high-speed blender, blend everything until smooth but not too runny. You may need to add a little more water to make this happen.
2. Pour into a jar (leaving at least a 4 cm gap at the top) and leave for at least 2hrs, but preferably another 2 days.
3. Once you start consuming place in a fridge.

Notes

› This 'cheese' smells really quite authentic, i.e., very cheesy!

Wild Garlic Pesto

Ingredients

700g-1kg wild garlic leaves
120g pine nuts, or chopped almonds
1 tbsp. salt
60ml filtered water
50-100g basil leaves
Salt and pepper to taste

Directions

1. Blend all the ingredients, except the water, in a food processor. (You can change the ratio of ingredients to your personal taste.)
2. Add the mixture to a jar, top up with the water so it comes just above the level of the mixture.
3. Place a small plate or weight over the top of the mixture so that it is all submerged.
4. Pop the lid on and put it in a cupboard for anywhere between 10 days and 2 months. Place in the fridge once opened.

Notes

› This can also be made with other wild greens too.
› You can add olive oil to the jar rather than brine/salted water, this will make a pesto closer to shop-bought pesto and one that you can use almost straight away.
› Don't pull up the wild garlic bulbs – the leaves (and flowers) are the best bit of wild garlic and, if you leave the bulbs, even more wild garlic will be there next year.
› This will keep for a year if kept in a cool, dark place and is a great addition to sourdough, pasta or even salads. This is one of my all-time favourite ferments!

Mayonnaise

Ingredients

1 egg yolk
1 tsp. raw apple cider vinegar
1 tsp. mustard
80-100ml of olive oil
1 tsp. of kombucha, kimchi or kraut juice
1 pinch of freshly ground pepper
½ tsp. sea salt
1-2 garlic cloves, crushed, for a garlic mayo (optional)

Directions

1. Add all but the olive oil to a bowl and whisk well.
2. Slowly add the olive oil a little at a time, whisking well between.
3. Once you have the desired consistency, stop adding oil and pour into a jar, making sure there is at least 2cm of space at the top of the jar.
4. Cover the jar with some muslin, cotton or a coffee filter and an elastic band.
5. Store away from direct sunlight, in a place not too hot or not too cold, on a plate or saucer (in case of leaks if you have overfilled), and leave for 1-3 days or until you see bubbles start to appear.
6. Store in the refrigerator until you need, but make sure you use it within 1 month.

Ketchup

Ingredients

500g tomato paste
3 tbsp. raw apple cider vinegar
1-2 tbsp. raw honey
1 small garlic clove, crushed
½ tsp. mustard powder
¼ tsp. allspice, ground

60ml of kombucha, kimchi or kraut juice
½ tsp. sea salt

Directions

1. Add all ingredients to a food processor and blend for a short time until well mixed (don't over blend).
2. Pour into a jar, making sure there is at least 2 cm's of space at the top of the jar.
3. Cover the jar with some muslin, cotton or a coffee filter and an elastic band.
4. Store away from direct sunlight, in a place not too hot or not too cold, on a plate or saucer (in case of leaks if you have overfilled), and leave for 3-5 days.
5. Store in the refrigerator until you need, but make sure you use it within 2 months.

Kombucha Mustard

Ingredients

Whole mustard seeds
Kombucha tea (to cover by at least 1 inch)
2 garlic cloves
1 heap tsp. Turmeric

1/2 tsp. paprika
1-2 tbsp. of lemon or lime juice (to taste)
1 tsp. sea salt

Directions

1. Fill a glass jar half full of mustard seeds and add salt and garlic.
2. Cover mustard seeds with kombucha tea, then add at least another inch of kombucha on top of this.
3. Cover the jar with some muslin and an elastic band.
4. Check the seeds after a few days and make sure that there is still excess kombucha tea above the seeds. If not, add a little more because the seeds will continue to swell.
5. After about two weeks the seeds will be soft and ready to blend.
6. Add everything in the jar to the blender (if there is not very much liquid you may want to add a little more kombucha).
7. Add the turmeric, paprika and lemon/lime and blend the whole lot until smooth, then put into a jar.
8. Use straight away, or leave in the fridge and use over the next couple of months.

Chili Sauce

Ingredients

3-4 chilies, chopped
3-4 red or orange peppers, chopped and de-seeded
2 white or red onions, peeled and de-seeded
2-4 garlic cloves, grated
3 tsp. of sea salt

Fresh, filtered water to fill jar, or kombucha, kimchi or kraut juice
1-2 tsp. chili powder or flakes (optional depending on your heat preference)
1-2 tsp of miso paste (optional)
2 tbsp. of seaweed flakes (optional)

Directions

1. Add all of the ingredients into a high-speed blender and blend until smooth.
2. Pour into a jar, making sure that there is at least a 2 cm air gap at the top of the jar or bottle.
3. Place wax paper on top to seal.
4. Store away from direct sunlight, in a place not too hot or not too cold, on a plate or saucer (in case of leaks if you have overfilled) with the lid loose, or remember to burp daily. Leave for 5 days.
5. Place in a fridge and start consuming when ready.

Mango Chutney

Ingredients

2 small mangoes, peeled, de-seeded and chopped
1 small red onion, finely chopped
4 cm's of fresh ginger, peeled and finely chopped
1 garlic clove, peeled and minced
1 tsp. chili flakes
1/2 tsp. curry powder
2 tbsp. of kombucha, kimchi or kraut juice
1 tsp. sea salt
Juice of 1 lime

Directions

1. Place all the ingredients in a bowl and mix well.
2. Pack it all down into a jar, if the liquid does not rise above the mango mixture then add a little filtered water until it does.
3. Place some wax paper, a boiled stone, a sterile weight of some sort or even a bag of salted water (the salt is there in case the bag splits) to weigh it all down
4. Store away from direct sunlight, in a place not too hot or not too cold, on a plate or saucer (in case of leaks if you have overfilled) with the lid loose, or remember to burp daily. Leave for 3 days.
5. Once you start consuming from the jar, put it in the fridge (this ferment will only last a week or two due to the high sugar content).

Zhug

Ingredients

10 chili peppers, de-steamed and chopped (traditionally done with green peppers, but I love the red ones)
1 bunch of fresh coriander, chopped
1 bunch of fresh parsley, chopped
12 garlic cloves, finely chopped
1 tsp. black pepper, freshly ground
1 tsp. coriander seeds, freshly ground
1 tsp cumin seeds, freshly ground
1 tsp. cardamom, freshly ground
Juice of 1 small lemon
1 tsp. of sea salt
50-70 ml of water
1 tsp. seaweeds flakes (optional)
1 tsp. of mustard seeds, freshly ground (optional)

Directions

1. Place all the ingredients (but just half the water to start with) into a food processor and blend to a paste. If it will not blend properly, add the other half of the water.
2. Pour into a jar, making sure that there is at least a 2 cm air gap at the top of the jar or bottle.
3. Place wax paper on top to seal.
4. Store away from direct sunlight, in a place not too hot or not too cold, on a plate or saucer (in case of leaks if you have overfilled) with the lid loose, or remember to burp daily. Leave for 5 days.
5. Place in a fridge and start consuming when ready.

Notes

› You can toast all the spices first for a slightly different flavour, but either way this recipe is a delight to the senses because it smells, looks and tastes amazing.

Kidney Bean Pate

Ingredients

100g of cooked kidney beans (or any cooked beans)
2 cloves of garlic
50-70ml of kombucha, kimchi or kraut juice
1 small onion, chopped
1 pinch of freshly ground pepper
½ tsp. of sea salt
½ tsp. of your favourite dried herbs (optional)

Directions

1. Add all ingredients into your food processor and blend until it looks like a pate.
2. If it's too thick, add a little bit more sauerkraut, kimchi juice or kombucha water.
3. Pour into a jar, making sure that there is at least a 2 cm air gap at the top of the jar.
4. Place wax paper on top to seal.
5. Cover the jar with muslin or cotton and an elastic band and leave on the counter out of direct sunlight for 3 days.
6. Place in a fridge and start consuming when ready.

Black Bean Miso

There are so many different miso recipes you can try. I don't eat soya, so I experimented with a lot of different ones and found, by far, that my favourite is back bean miso, so here's the recipe for that…

Ingredients
800g of black beans
1kg of koji rice
100ml of black bean water
200g of sea salt, plus more for sprinkling on top
100ml of black bean water

Directions

1. Cook the beans in a pressure cooker for 20mins (or in saucepan until tender if you don't have a pressure cooker). Allow beans to cool down.
2. Put everything, apart from the salt for sprinkling, into a food processor and blend.
3. Put everything into a large jar and push down so there are no gaps anywhere.
4. Sprinkle salt on top to completely cover the mixture.
5. Put some wax paper on top to completely cover the surface and then weigh this down with crock weights or a stone (making sure these are sterile).
6. Store in a cool, dark place for at least 3 months, but preferably 6–9 months.
7. Keep refrigerated once you start using it.
8. Black Bean Miso Notes
9. It's quite likely mold will form on top of your miso, this is normal and you can just scrape the mold off before you start using it.
10. You can use soya, split peas, kidney beans, rice and more to make miso.
11. Some people use a little bit of a previous batch to get the next batch 'going', you can do this but it is not necessary.

Tapenade

Ingredients

300g pitted unpasteurized olives (I use olives that don't look too pretty)
2-4 garlic cloves, chopped
2 tbsp. olive oil
2 tbsp. of kombucha, kimchi or kraut juice
1 tbsp. sea salt
1-2 handfuls of capers (optional)

Directions

1. Place all ingredients in a food processor and blend well, making sure to scrape the side of the processor.
2. Pour into a jar, making sure that there is at least a 2 cm air gap at the top of the jar.
3. Place wax paper on top to seal.
4. Cover the jar with muslin or cotton and an elastic band, leave on the counter out of direct sunlight for 5–7 days.
5. Place in a fridge and start consuming when ready.

Notes

› Many people don't realise olives in themselves are a fermented food (as long as they have not been pasterised), so this is an easy fermented food to consume even without turning it into a Tapenade.

Honey Garlic

Ingredients

200g whole garlic cloves, peeled and crushed (or black or blue elderberries – strictly no stems or leaves)
1L raw honey

Directions

1. Place garlic into a large jar.
2. Add enough honey to completely cover all the garlic.
3. Put the lid on the jar loosely and store in a cool dark place (but nowhere that might have honey-loving ants around).
4. Once a day, tighten the lid and shake well, then place back in its position with the lid loose again.
5. After a week you can stop shaking it, but leave for at least a month before consuming.

Notes

› Sometimes your garlic will turn blue/green, this is perfectly normal and safe to consume.
› Some people are concerned about botulism with garlic recipes like this. Check it's pH is less than 4.6 if you are concerned, because botulism can't live below this pH.
› When using elderberries instead of garlic, add enough honey to make sure there is at least 1 inch of honey over the top of the elderberries. You need to be careful when straining the berries (do not consume them). Take 1 tsp. whenever there are a lot of colds/coughs/flu around. DO NOT use red elderberries and make sure there are no stems or leaves in the honey mixture, as these are toxic.

Spicy Lemons

Ingredients

6-8 lemons (enough to fill your chosen jar)
1 tbsp. sea salt per lemon
1/2 tsp. cayenne pepper, ground
1/4-1/2 tsp. chili powder

Directions

1. Top and tail lemons and then slice into quarters.
2. Add salt/spice mix into the middle of each lemon, then place the lemons one by one into a jar upright.
3. Wedge lemons in tightly so they don't move around.
4. Pour in water to cover all of the lemons.
5. Make sure everything is below the level of the water, if it is not add a little extra water until it is.
6. Make sure there is at least 2 cm's of empty space at the top of the jar.
7. If the lemons are not wedged in and float to the top, then weigh down with a sterilized pebble or a kitchen weight of some description.
8. Store away from direct sunlight, in a place not too hot or not too cold, with the lid loose. Leave for at least 2 months, but preferably 6 months.

Breakfast Ferment

Ingredients

3 apples or pears, chopped into smallish pieces
2 handfuls of seeds of your choice (I like pumpkin and sunflowers seeds)
2 handfuls of nuts of your choice (I like hazel nuts and cashews)
2 handfuls of dried fruits of your choice (I like raisins and sultanas)
1-2 tsp. of cinnamon
1 tsp. of nutmeg
1 tbsp. sea salt

Directions

1. Put all the ingredients in a bowl and mix well.
2. Pack tightly into jars and fill with water to cover the ingredients.
3. Place the lid loosely on top and leave on the side, but not in direct sunlight for 3 days.
4. Tighten the lid and shake once daily.
5. Now it's ready to eat, so refrigerate and consume within 2 weeks.

Notes

› Place in the fridge after no more than 4 days because the fruit will turn the ferment fizzy after this time (fruity ferments don't keep as long but are soooo good).
› The great thing about this recipe is you can use just about any dried fruits, seeds and nuts you like, so it doesn't matter what you have in the cupboard.
› This fruity breakfast ferment recipe couldn't be easier, and can also be eaten as pudding with a little ice cream or cold custard.

Spicy Pineapple

Ingredients

1 pineapple, peeled and cut into large chunks or circles to fit jar
1 small chili, thinly sliced
1 tbsp. kraut or kimchi juice
1 heap tbsp. sea salt
Filtered water to fill your jar

Directions

1. Put pineapple and chilies into your jar.
2. Add salt and kraut/kimchi juice.
3. Fill jar with water, making sure everything is covered but ensuring there is a 2cm gap at the top of the jar.
4. Place a lid on loosely and leave on the counter to ferment for 2 to 4 days.
5. Refrigerate after this time and consume within 2 weeks.

Fermented Drinks

Kombucha

Kombucha is an ancient, strong fermented/probiotic drink made from sweet tea and using a scoby (symbiotic culture of bacteria and yeast)/mother/mushroom. It is thought that Kombucha originated in Northern China and spread like tea along the Silk Road. It is believed to date back to 220 B.C. when even then it was prized for its healing properties. Kombucha is a non-alcoholic drink that contains vitamins, amino acids and other nutrients, so it's great all round for digestive health and thus health of the whole body and mind.

Ingredients

500ml tea (cooled)
3 tbsp. white sugar

1 scoby / mushroom / mother in 100-150ml of kombucha tea from your last batch

Directions

1. Pour 500ml of boiling water over a black, white, green teabag (or a handful of high tannin plant leaves – see notes below) in a large jar, add sugar and stir until dissolved.
2. Allow to brew until cold and then remove the teabag/leaves.
3. Add your scoby and 100-150ml of a previous batch of kombucha tea to the jar (this is the liquid in the packet of a new scoby – if you are starting for the first time like this).
4. Cover the top of the jar securely with some muslin, a coffee filter or a piece of cotton and an elastic band, as your scoby needs to breathe.
5. Place the jar on the kitchen side, away from direct sunlight and the cooker.
6. Let your kombucha brew for 5-10 days (depending on how hot it is – in the summer mine usually takes 5 days and in the winter 7-8 days), but note that the less time you leave it, the more sugar and caffeine will be left it in. It should not taste too sweet or too vinegary when ready to drink.
7. Another kombucha scoby (a baby) will start to form on the top of the liquid and will look like thick slime to start with. You can leave the new and the old scoby in the kombucha with each batch until they are too thick. Once you have a minimum of 1cm of thickness, remove half.
8. After 5-10 days, pour all but 100–150ml of the batch out to drink and make some more sweet tea. Add cooled sweet tea and again leave for 5–10 days.
9. Keep repeating this process for regular batches of kombucha. You can slowly increase the quantity of water, sugar and tea with each batch until you have the right amount to last you between batches.
10. You can drink your kombucha as it is (keeping it in the fridge between drinks) or you can do a second fermentation where you flavour it.

11. Pick your favorite flavors (lemon and ginger, hibiscus, berries, elderflower & lemon, lime, mint, etc) and add this to the kombucha you have poured off to drink. Put it in a bottle, put it in the fridge and leave overnight.
12. The following day open the bottle and taste. If it's strong enough, then remove the flavourings and start to consume. If not, leave for another day.
13. If you want fizzy kombucha, then pick something to flavour it that has natural sugars (berries for instance) and put into the fridge with the lid tight.
14. The following day when you open it there should be some fizz in it. Do not leave for longer than a day, the sugars in the fruit will continue the fermentation process and the bottle could go 'boom'. If in any doubt, use plastic bottles and check twice daily.

Kombucha Notes

› There are concerns from people about the caffeine and sugar in the drink, but by the time it is ready to drink (5 to 10 days, depending on how hot it is) there should be little to no caffeine or sugar left. Kombucha needs tannins to do its job, so it can be made with black, white or green tea (loose or tea bags), or any plants high in tannins like olive (my preferred option), raspberry, verbena, oak or vine leaves (so then there is no caffeine to start with anyway).
› It's really hard to kill off your kombucha scoby. Many people think they have because it does not float, has stringy bits, has black bits or looks odd (well odder than it normally does) in some way. But, in most cases, it's still alive and kicking.
› Putting your kombucha to sleep – If you are going away or want a Kombucha break, then put your kombucha in the fridge in its sweet tea (you can leave it in here for months, even a year if the lid is on loose).
› Sometimes you may forget your kombucha and it will become vinegary. I don't recommend drinking it then because it's very acidic, but you can use it as vinegar (add it into salad dressings etc for an additional probiotic kick), or use as a wonderful, natural weed killer in your garden, or to clean the drains in your home.
› You can use extra scobys up by using them for a base for some skin care products, composting them, giving them away, dehydrating them

when mixed with fruit as fruit leathers, feeding them to your chickens, or using them as band aids (keeping them in a jar in the fridge for when you have cuts, stings, bites etc as they are anti-bacterial and great for external use on the body, as well as internal use).

- The scoby is actually a biproduct of the fermentation process and not the actual thing that makes your drink. Therefore, the liquid from a previous batch is so important because this is full of the good bacteria we want to make another batch. You can start making a batch of kombucha with only a scoby or only the liquid, but it's better to have both if you want to be sure of being successful. You will often see scobies growing in fermented drinks in health food shops, you can be sure these are unpasteurized then!
- Shop-bought kombuchas are often pasteurized (cooked, so they have very little or no probiotics left) and full of sugar. You can tell if they are pasteurized as they will usually be set on the shelf and not in the fridge. Fermented foods and drinks are not usually self-stable, because they are still fermenting as this temperature.

Water Kefir

Water kefir (or Tibicos) is a traditional fermented/probiotic drink made with water, sugar and gelatinous "grains" from the prickly pear cactus in Mexico.

Ingredients

60g organic sugar
200ml hot water
720ml cold water

4 tbsp. water kefir grains
2-3 slices of lemon, 8 raisins or 1 eggshell (optional)

Directions

1. Put the sugar and hot water into a large jar and allow to dissolve.
2. Top up with cold water.
3. Add the water kefir grains.
4. If you feel there are not many minerals in your water, then add lemon, raisins or eggshells too.
5. Secure some muslin, cotton or a coffee filter over the top of the jar with a rubber band.
6. Let it ferment for 2-3 days; a little shorter if you prefer it sweet (with higher sugar content) and a little longer if you prefer it slightly more sour (lower sugar content).
7. When it reaches your preferred taste, use a plastic sieve (metal items can damage the grains) to separate the grains from the liquid. Then put the grains directly into a new lot of sugar water (as above) to start a new batch.
8. You can now drink the liquid as it is, but make sure to store it in the fridge to prevent further fermentation.
9. Or you can do a second ferment to add more flavour and fizz to your kefir. Add juiced fruit, or even vegetables like beetroot, to the kefir drink you have poured off, and put it in a jar or bottle and close the lid firmly. This will allow the kefir to get fizzy like a flavoured soda. Leave this for another 24 hours and then store in the fridge when it is at your preferred taste.

Notes

› The grains eat up all the sugar and you are left with a uber-strong probiotic drink instead.
› You'll know if your Kefir is happy as it will grow lots of new grains quickly, you will see them floating around often too.
› If your water kefir does not seem to be doing very much it could be because you are leaving it too long between batches, or there is not enough sugar or minerals in the water.
› Don't ferment Kombucha and Kefir too close to each other because they can get cross-contaminated, and you can end up a spider-web like mould all over one or both of them.

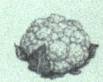

Milk Kefir

Milk kefir is a fermented/probiotic milk drink, like a thin yogurt, which is made from kefir grains, a specific type of mesophilic symbiotic culture. The drink originates in the Northern Caucasus and the former USSR. It is prepared by inoculating cow, goat or sheep milk.

Ingredients

900ml raw milk (or organic whole milk)
1-2 tbsp. milk kefir grains (these are not the same grains as water kefirs)

Directions

1. Place your kefir grains in the jar and add the milk.
2. Stir with a wooden spoon (remember, no metal as this can harm the grains), cover and secure with muslin and an elastic band. Leave at room temperature to culture for up to 1-2 days, depending on preferred taste or room temperature.
3. A shorter fermentation time will mean a milder flavour, and a longer one will mean a stronger and sourer flavour.
4. Once your kefir is done culturing, remove the grains (this is usually easier with your hands as it can be quite thick). Store the kefir milk in the refrigerator and begin another batch with the grains.

Notes

› Many people who feel they have a dairy intolerance are often OK with consuming milk in this way. Not only that, but it can help with other intolerances too.
› You can use kefir to make milkshakes, yogurt and smoothies, or just flavour with fruit too.

Ginger Bug

Ingredients

5 cm of ginger grated
3 tbsp. of sugar
250ml of water

Directions

1. Put half the grated ginger, 2 tbsp. of the sugar and the water into a medium sized sterile jar and shake well. Take lid off and cover with muslin or cotton and an elastic band.
2. Put in a warm place and shake frequently (every time you look at it) for 24hrs.
3. After 24hrs you should see bubbles. If you do not see bubbles, then add a little more sugar and ginger and keep shaking for another 24hrs.
4. You ginger bug is ready to make ginger beer with. If you don't want to use it right now, then you can either continue feeding and shaking it every few days, or put it in the fridge where it will go to 'sleep' for a bit (it will need feeding again as soon as you remove it from the fridge).

Notes

› You need to make a ginger bug to make ginger beer or other drinks, like fizzy orange, lemon, lime or even beetroot drinks.

› It's your starter that you can make as and when needed, or keep going between batches for a quicker next batch.

Ginger Beer

Ginger beer is thought to date back to 1,700 B.C., was created in Yorkshire, England and is not actually a beer at all!

Ingredients

20cm of ginger (or turmeric or a mix of both), grated
375ml sugar
2 lemons, juiced

6L of water
1 ginger bug

Directions

1. Put grated ginger and 2L of water into a large pan, and bring to the boil. Once boiling, simmer for 30mins.
2. Take off the heat, add the sugar and stir until dissolved.
3. Strain the grated ginger from the liquid and add the other 4L of cold water.
4. The liquid should be cool now, add the ginger bug and lemon juice and stir. Pour this all into a large plastic bucket or glass jar (not metal). Put lid loosely on and leave for 24hrs in a warm place.
5. After 24hrs it should smell like ginger beer and be bubbling. If not, then leave another 24hrs.
6. Put into plastic bottles, but leave 3 inches at least of empty space at the top.
7. Leave in a cool place for at least 3 days, preferably 6, and then put in the fridge (be careful when opening as it may be lively).
8. All or most of the sugar will be eaten up by the fermentation process.

Notes

› Your ginger bug must be bubbly when you go to use it, otherwise the ginger beer will not work.
› You can make other fizzy 'beer's / drinks in the same way as above, but with either substituting the ginger for things like beetroot or by substituting the first 2L of water with something like juiced oranges or grapefruit. Note the high fruit content in these will make it ferment quicker and they will not last as long.

Turmeric Mead

Mead, also named nectar of the Gods because it's created from fermenting honey and fruits, dates back to 7,000 B.C. It's also where the name 'honeymoon' is thought to come from, as it was used to celebrate Weddings.

Ingredients

4L water (filtered)
250g turmeric root, or a mix of turmeric & ginger, sliced thinly or grated
1kg raw honey
1-2 tsp. black peppercorns (optional)

Directions

1. Place turmeric in a jar with black peppercorns, if desired.
2. Mix the honey with the turmeric and stir.
3. The little bit of juice that the honey pulls from the turmeric is enough to start fermentation.
4. Stir the mixture once a day for a couple of weeks, until it's bubbly.
5. Then transfer it to a large glass jar that can hold 5L and add the water.
6. Mix well, until the honey is thoroughly dissolved.
7. Put the lid on loose, or put an airlock on the bottle.
8. Ferment for several months, until all signs of bubbling stop. You can drink it now, though it will still be quite sweet and low alcohol. Or continue to ferment it for several more months, which will increase the alcohol level.
9. Strain out the turmeric slices.
10. Drink it now, or bottle and store in the fridge or in bottles that can let out the gas.

Notes

› You can make mead in the above way with lots of seasonal produce. I like orange (slices) and raisin mead, or lime (slices) and mint flavour.
› If the gas cannot escape you will end up with a fizzy mead (some people like this), but you can also end up with an explosion, so be careful about this.

Tepache

Ingredients

The peel of 1 medium pineapple
2L of filtered water
200g brown sugar
1 cinnamon stick

Directions

1. Rinse the whole pineapple.
2. Cut off the top and compost it.
3. Remove the peel, but leave some of the fruit on the inside of it.
4. Remove the core, then add the peels and core to a large jar.
5. Dissolve the sugar in the filtered water and add to the jar.
6. Add a boiled stone, a sterile weight of some sort or even a bag of salted water (the salt is there in case the bag splits) to weigh it all down.
7. Make sure everything is covered, but save a 2cm gap at the top of the jar.
8. Cover with muslin (or leave lid loose) and leave on the counter at room temperature for 3 – 4 days.
9. Strain, bottle and leave in fridge.

Notes

› A scum may appear on the top of this ferment, this is fine, either mix back in or skim off (whichever you prefer). You can shake this daily to reduce the scum building up.
› Most or all of the processed sugar will be eaten up by the fermentation process.
› Due to the fruit's high sugar content, this ferment won't keep long, consume within one week.
› It does not smell good but will taste awesome.

Beetroot Kvass

Kvass is a traditional fermented Slavic & Baltic beverage commonly made from rye bread, dating from before 996 A.D. However, these days many fermenters are making beetroot Kvass, which comes from Ukraine. It's a great fermented drink to make because you don't need a 'starter' that you have to feed and keep alive between fermenting batches.

Ingredients

2-4 fresh beetroot
40-60ml of kombucha, kimchi or kraut juice
1-4 cm of grated ginger, or any herbs or spices of your choosing (optional)

1 tbsp. sea salt
Filtered water, to cover

Directions

1. Wash beets. Leave skin on if organic, or peel off skin if not organic.
2. Chop beets into small cubes and place in a large jar.
3. Add kombucha, kimchi or kraut juice, salt and ginger or spices.
4. Fill jar with filtered water to cover beets well.
5. Cover with muslin (or leave lid loose) and leave on the counter at room temperature for 2 weeks, or until you start to see bubbles.
6. Give it a stir every day.
7. Drain beets etc from liquid and transfer to fridge.
8. You can eat the leftover beets as they are in salads, or blend and make a dip with them. The beetroot is filled with probiotics.

Notes

› Adding sauerkraut (or the juice of any other ferment) can speed up the fermentation time and reduces the risk of it going bad.

Christmas Kvass

Ingredients

1 small apple or pear, sliced
½-1 orange, sliced (with the peel still on)
1 good handful of raisins
1 tbsp. of honey or maple syrup
½-1 tsp. cinnamon, ground

½-1 tsp. ginger, ground or fresh
¼-1 tsp. nutmeg or all-spice (optional)
Also optional: persimmon, pomegranate or any other winter fruit

Directions

1. Put all of the items in a large jar, filling halfway.
2. Fill with spring water almost to the top (leaving 2 cm's at least).
3. Put the lid on tightly and shake well, then release the lid and leave loose.
4. Shake every day for 3 days and then open.
5. Drain, bottle and leave in the fridge.
6. Consume within a few days, because even in the fridge it will continue to ferment quickly due to the high sugar content of the fruits.

Grapefruit Juice

Ingredients

700ml fresh squeezed grapefruit juice
300ml filtered water
½ tsp. of kombucha, kimchi or kraut juice
¼ tsp. sea salt

Directions

1. Pour juice and water into a large jar.
2. Add sauerkraut, kimchi or kombucha and salt.
3. Cover tightly, shake well, and leave at room temperature for 24-48 hours.
4. Be careful when opening and never leave for longer than 48hrs, as it may go 'boom'.

Apple Juice

Ingredients

9 organic apples
1 tsp. of kombucha, kimchi or kraut juice
¼ tsp. sea salt

Directions

1. Juice the apples, skimming off as much foam as possible.
2. Add sauerkraut, kimchi juice or kombucha and salt to the juice.
3. Pour into a large jar.
4. Put the lid on the jar tightly and shake well, leave at room temperature for 2 days.
5. Be careful opening and never leave for longer than 48hrs, as it may go 'boom'.

Apple Cider Vinegar

The use of apple cider vinegar can be traced back to Hippocrates times, when even then it was sworn by for its medicinal benefits.

Ingredients

6-10 organic apples (whole or scraps)
Water (to fill your jar)

Directions

1. Rinse apples/scraps and cut into large chunks.
2. Put the apples in the bowl and cover with something breathable, allowing the apples to go brown.
3. Put the apples into your jar and cover with water.
4. Cover the jar with muslin and leave in a dark place for 2 months.
5. Strain the apple pieces and any scum from the liquid, bottle in an airtight container, and keep in a cool, dark place.

Fermented Skin Care

It's becoming more popular to add fermented drinks to skin and hair care products. The reason for this is that the benefits these amazing drinks have for our insides, can also happen on our outsides too. They can supply the skin and hair with probiotics, removing pesky bacteria and fungus, and add nutrients, and even amino acids, to the skin and hair. They can also provide a protection for the skin and strengthen the skin's metabolism, making it stronger and healthier.

Some people use extra Kombucha scobies and place them on their face, as a face mask. I would not recommend this for sensitive skin, but it makes total sense it would help the health of your skin when used topically like this. I also mentioned earlier in this book that you can use your scoby as a band aid, due to its anti-bacterial properties.

Kombucha Toner

Ingredients

100ml of kombucha tea
4 drops of tea tree essential oil
2 drops of lavender essential oil

Directions

1. Add ingredients to a jar and shake well.
2. For sensitive skin, use Kombucha water that is no more than 1 week old as it can become acidic and harsh for the skin.
3. Store in the refrigerator and use within a couple of weeks.

Kefir Face Mask for Combination Skin

Ingredients

2 tbsp. milk kefir
1 small cucumber
1 tsp. honey for oily skin, or 1 tsp. olive oil for dry skin (optional)

Directions

1. Juice the cucumber.
2. Mix cucumber juice with kefir (and honey or olive oil).
3. Apply mask to face and leave for 20 minutes.
4. Rinse with warm water.

Kombucha Face Mask

Ingredients

1 tbsp. of bentonite clay
2 tsp. of Kombucha water

Directions

1. Mix to form a paste.
2. Apply to face liberally.
3. Leave for 10 mins.
4. Rinse off.

Face & Body Scrub

Ingredients

1-½ tsp. apple cider vinegar
6 ground almonds
2 tsp. sugar
3 tsp. of raw honey
1 tsp. aloe vera gel

Directions

1. Add everything to a bowl and stir well.
2. Add to wet skin and scrub well.
3. Rinse off.
4. Store in refrigerator for up to 1 week.

Kombucha Hair Tonic

Ingredients

200ml Kombucha tea
1 handful fresh rosemary
1-2 drops of tea tree oil (optional for dandruff)

Directions

1. Add all ingredients to a jar and shake well.
2. Allow to sit for 3 days, shaking well each day.
3. Add after washing hair, but leave tonic on until hair is dried.
4. Store in refrigerator and use within 2 weeks.

Rice Water Shampoo

Ingredients

200g rice
450ml filtered water
150ml chamomile tea
60ml aloe vera juice

225ml liquid castile soap
Optional: 20-40 drops of lavender essential oil

Directions

1. Put rice in a bowl and rinse well.
2. Add warm water, stir and cover the bowl. Allow to soak for 30mins (stirring halfway through).
3. Strain the water from the rice, cover the water and allow to sit until you see fermenting bubbles appear (24–48hrs).
4. Add soap, chamomile tea, aloe vera and lavender oil.
5. Shake well before use.

Notes

› This recipe must be kept in the fridge and used within 1 week.
› You can boil the rice after making this recipe to consume as normal.

Scalp Scrub

Ingredients

1 tsp. raw apple cider vinegar (see ACV recipe earlier in this book)
1 tsp. coconut oil, melted
1 tsp. raw honey
70g sea salt
Optional: 15 drops of any citrus essential oil

Directions

1. Add everything to a bowl and stir well.
2. Add to wet hair and scrub scalp.
3. Leave on hair for 5 mins and then rinse well with your chosen shampoo.
4. Store in the refrigerator and use within 1 week.

Fermented Cleaning Products

Here are a couple of fermented cleaning options I wanted to share with you, to show you that you can make fermented, probiotic and thus healthy versions of many quite toxic things we use in our homes. These cleaners won't only clean, but will leave all the good bacteria we need around us behind.

Surface Cleaner

Ingredients

Juice of 1 lemon
100ml of raw apple cider vinegar
1 orange, sliced
1L filtered water

Directions

1. Place all ingredients in a large jar and shake well.
2. Add a piece of muslin, cotton or a coffee filter to the top of the jar with an elastic band.
3. Leave in a cool, dark place for 1 month, then strain and bottle the liquid.
4. Keep in the refrigerator between uses to keep for longer.

Oven Cleaner

Ingredients

750ml of filtered water
150ml kombucha tea
100g baking soda

Directions

1. Mix the liquids and, once well mixed, add the baking soda (not before).
2. Apply directly to greasy areas of your oven and scrub.
3. Left over Kombucha (that has turned to vinegar) is an amazing way to clean drains and kill weeds too!

Art & Obsession

Life will never quite be the same once you start fermenting!

It tickles the creative juices and taste buds, whilst assisting all systems of the body, the mind, energy levels and, well, pretty much all of life. It's an amazing way to preserve food, to get more from our food and to use up food that's on its 'way out'.

Tinkering away in the kitchen, trying out recipes, figuring out ways to use up surplus vegetables, finding whole new areas of fermenting have been some of my most enjoyable moments. When I think of the hundreds and hundreds of hours spent on fermenting, not one minute of this was wasted time. Not even when the odd batch goes 'funky', not even then.

Fermenting has been a key factor in my improved health over the years and has also given me so much more. A love of food again, a passion for teaching and a purpose in life.

I've always found time to ferment with friends, to teach workshops to the community and to grow foods that I know I can ferment. Time is always found for fermenting in all these forms, and I notice not always for other things.

If the fermenting obsession gets you too, then I would love to hear from you. The more people fermenting the happier and healthier this World would be.

I feel we are being called back to more traditional ways of doing things now, ways that aren't pushy, achiever-driven, but natural, nurturing and nourishing. There is an ease, a slowness and a healing in these more traditional processes that have been lost.

I hope you find your way back to a simple, traditional and more nourishing life, and you share what you find too, Faith xx

www.ingramcontent.com/pod-product-compliance
Lightning Source LLC
Chambersburg PA
CBHW051601010526
44118CB00023B/2774